FAREWELL to CALM

The New Normal Survival Guide

JOHN CRACE

First published by Guardian Faber in 2021
Guardian Faber is an imprint of Faber & Faber Limited,
Bloomsbury House, 74–77 Great Russell Street,
London WC1B 3DA
Guardian is a registered trade mark of
Guardian News & Media Ltd,
Kings Place, 90 York Way, London N1 9GU

Printed in the UK by CPI Group (UK) Ltd, Croydon CR0 4YY

A CIP record for this book is available from the British Library

ISBN 978–1–78335–244–9

2 4 6 8 10 9 7 5 3 1

For Robbie and Laila

Introduction

It was almost enough to make you miss Theresa May. At least there had been an integrity to her incompetence. You could count on her to be doing the wrong thing for the right reason. And her speeches did generally conform to normal syntax, even if they were almost entirely meaningless.

But with May's resignation and the election of Boris Johnson as the new Conservative leader – and hence prime minister – in July 2019, it felt as if we were in the political Wild West. A one-man amoral no-go zone, whose prime motivation was his own survival and who could only talk in bursts of white noise.

Johnson had breezed through life, failing effortlessly upwards while happily trashing the lives of all those with whom he came in contact. For him, being the prime minister was merely a position of entitlement rather than of responsibility. The ideal job for someone predisposed to laziness and arrogance, someone for whom the idea of any preparation was an unthinkable admission of failure.

So it's fair to say Boris was in for something of a wake-up call. Not least in his first four months in the job, when just about everything that could go wrong, did. As ever, it was Brexit that exposed not only the fault lines in the House of Commons, but also those within the Conservative Party itself. Johnson had always been adamant that he would 'die in a ditch' if the UK had not left the European Union by 31 October, but mostly he looked as if he was dying on his feet.

It was nothing short of chaos. First, there had been the case of the five-week prorogation that never was, ordered by the Queen in late August on Boris's advice. Boris had insisted that the suspension was what parliament really wanted, as it would give MPs plenty of free time to get on with other things. And if parliament had not wanted to be prorogued, it would have made its feelings clear through interpretive dance. The reality was that Johnson – and Dominic Cummings, his chief political adviser – wanted to cut short the amount of time the Commons would have to debate the Brexit bill. After all, if parliament wasn't sitting, then there was no way the government could be defeated.

Despite Johnson insisting he had done nothing wrong, the Supreme Court unanimously ruled that the government had acted illegally in calling for the prorogation. Parliament was back in business the next day, and not long after Her Majesty was in the Lords delivering a Queen's Speech that everyone knew was just fantasy, an election manifesto at best. The Queen made no effort to disguise her feelings at being misled over the legality of the prorogation – something to which she had been obliged to give her assent – and her delivery of the speech felt more like an exorcism, a desperate purge of the toxic waste that had been forced on her by a prime minister she had come to detest.

Then there were all those votes in the Commons that he had lost, starting with the bill to rule out a no-deal Brexit. Twenty-one Tory MPs, including Ken Clarke, Philip Hammond and Nicholas Soames, had voted against the government by backing the motion their party had always said it didn't want. Their punishment was to have the whip withdrawn, leaving Boris with a majority of more than minus 40.

Johnson had also three times demanded a general election he had repeatedly said he didn't want, but none of the opposition leaders obliged. Under the Fixed-Term Parliaments Act of 2011, the government needed a two-thirds majority to get its way. It didn't even come close. As far as the opposition was concerned, Boris could go whistle. If it was all the same to him, they would wait until the Queen had given royal assent to the bill blocking a no-deal Brexit. His reputation for dishonesty preceded him.

Alongside the many lost votes was the betrayal of Northern Ireland's Democratic Unionist Party. At the DUP's conference in November 2018, Johnson had said no British Conservative government could sign up to regulatory checks and customs controls along the Irish

Sea. To do so would put the whole of the Union at risk. But now he had agreed a deal that did just that.

'We leave whole and entire,' he had declared. Apart from Northern Ireland. People would say he had thrown the DUP under a bus, but that wasn't fair. He had thrown them under a train. Far more efficient. He had done away with the temporary backstop by turning it into a permanent full stop. Genius. And remarkably, the hardline Tory Brexiteers of the European Research Group, who had always insisted they would stand by the DUP's demands for Northern Ireland, found that they could dump them too.

On and on the chaos went, with the government losing vote after vote and the Commons even sitting on a Saturday. Nor was it just the Tories who were confused. Labour, under the leadership of Jeremy Corbyn, was also confused. It both wanted an election and didn't want an election. It wanted an election because that's what opposition parties were supposed to want, but it also didn't want one because the polls indicated Labour would be resoundingly beaten. It also wanted to get Brexit done, but had no idea what version of Brexit it was that it wanted to get done.

The Tories, meanwhile, wanted an election, but didn't know how to get one or when. They would also quite like Johnson's Brexit deal to pass, while secretly wishing they had voted for Theresa May's rather better deal when they had had the chance. What was even weirder was *that this was the new normal and no one found any of this to be the slightest bit odd.*

But something had to give, and in the end it was Labour. With Johnson having secured a Brexit extension beyond 31 October, Corbyn instructed his MPs to vote for a general election in December. It turned out that no one was surprised or bothered that the prime minister hadn't kept his promise to die in a ditch. For the first time in months, both Boris and Cummings began to relax. They could see that the end was in sight.

The Tory campaign kept things simple: a three-word slogan of 'Get Brexit Done', a promise to be the 'People's Government', a commitment to levelling up the disparity in income and prospects around the country, and a pledge to build 40 new hospitals.

And things became simpler still when Nigel Farage, whose Brexit Party had won the European elections in May, chose to stand down all 317 of his candidates who had been due to contest Tory-held seats. The rationale was that Boris's deal was good enough, and he didn't want to take the risk of splitting the pro-Brexit vote and allowing Labour to sneak up on the rails. The net effect was that Nigel saw his party plummet from 17% to 4% in the opinion polls. Call it hubris, but it was Nigel who turned the Nigel Party into an irrelevance.

Meanwhile, Labour struggled to make any headway. It never fully shook off allegations of anti-Semitism within the party, while Corbyn's personal ratings were consistently disastrous. Even two press conferences held to expose leaked information that the Tories were planning to privatise the NHS and put a hard border down the Irish Sea amounted to nothing. Voters had never really expected Johnson to tell the truth, so the revelations were greeted with general indifference.

This would be less of an election and more of an unpopularity contest. Boris and Corbyn were widely disliked and mistrusted throughout the country. All that was at stake was which leader was hated the least. It was a race that Johnson won at a canter, with a landslide majority of 80 seats. The country was sick of Brexit and just wanted it over and done with. It was also sick of the old politics and wanted a prime minister who would do things differently. No one really expected Johnson to deliver on all his promises, but they were less worried about that than the promises on which Labour might deliver.

Boris duly celebrated the election of the 'People's Government' by elevating Nicky Morgan and Zac Goldsmith to the House of Lords and including them both in his first cabinet. How things change. There had been a time when Morgan had been a thorn in Theresa May's side, insisting that the only good Brexit deal was one in which the UK remained in the single market and the customs union. Now she was fully signed up to Johnson's hard Brexit. As was Goldsmith, once he had resolved the matter of his previous non-dom tax status.

As for Boris, he went off to Mustique to stay in a £15,000-per-week beach hut for the new year with his girlfriend, Carrie Symonds. We never did get to find out who had footed the bill for the holiday. In the Register of Members' Interests, Johnson listed David Ross, one of the founders of Carphone Warehouse, as the good Samaritan. But Ross later denied it had been him, saying only that he had helped the prime minister locate suitable accommodation. Attempting to find out who had paid for Boris's treats would prove a feature of his time in office.

Still, Boris did keep his promise on one thing. He did get Brexit done. With an 80-seat majority and all the Tory MPs – even the ones who had opposed it – fully on board with Johnson's Brexit vision, the bill went through with little opposition in parliament. Only the Scottish National Party and the Lib Dems put up any real resistance, and they were a minority Boris found easy to ignore. Anyone who even questioned what form the future arrangement with the EU would take – something that needed to be agreed by the end of the year – was sent to a re-education camp.

For Johnson, it had been a dream start to 2020. His ratings were consistently high, and Labour was preoccupied with a leadership contest after its worst general election result in the best part of 80 years. There seemed to be little that could go wrong. Certainly in the short term. He even found time to deliver a triumphalist speech in

Greenwich celebrating Britain's new trading relations with the rest of the world. Meanwhile, over in China, people were beginning to die from a new disease known as the coronavirus . . .

Boris Johnson goes missing in action on his big Brexit day

31 JANUARY 2020

Just imagine a country about to take a giant leap into the unknown. A future sold on the basis of promises that no one is certain can be kept. Now imagine the person least suitable to be prime minister at this time. A man whose entire career has been built on lies, deceit and self-destruction. A narcissist whose concentration span barely extends to the end of a senten— On second thoughts, don't bother. You've got him already.

There are a couple of ways of interpreting Boris Johnson's three-minute cameo posted on his Facebook page at 10 p.m. Neither shows the prime minister in a particularly good light. The first and the most obvious is that Boris really doesn't give much of a toss. He's got what he wanted and can now barely be arsed to go through the motions. His usual lethal combination of boredom and terminal laziness.

Any half-decent prime minister – and bizarrely, Theresa May now almost falls into this category – would have realised that Brexit day was a time to really up their game. To make a live, sincere address to the nation. One that properly acknowledged the significance of the occasion. Boris, not so much. He couldn't trust himself not to screw up a live broadcast – didn't he even have a party inside No. 10 already arranged? – so he did a quick pre-record the day before. Nor could he be bothered to do more than scribble down a few thoughts off the top of his head. Would this do? It would have to.

The second interpretation is perhaps the more telling. Because there are countless giveaways that Boris is actually embarrassed about what he has done. Think about it this way. How was the prime minister choosing to spend Brexit night? By bunkering down inside No. 10 with a handful of staffers, while a light show that none of the public was allowed in to see flickered mournfully on the outside of the building.

He did so because he didn't dare show his face – not even to go on TV – and take ownership of a Brexit that has been hewn in his own image. Shambolic and a bit clueless. Because deep down Boris has never really been a true believer.

Brexit was an ill-fitting carapace he had worn to get into power. He'd never really thought anyone would believe the lies he'd told. It was a game that had suddenly become all too real. The fun had stopped, but he couldn't. Now he was expected to take responsibility for what he had done, he just wanted to hide. The mask of denial and self-deception had momentarily slipped and the Supreme Showman was too ashamed to be seen.

The handheld hostage video opens with a shot of the No. 10 front door, which is as close to reassurance and gravitas as we get. Then we cut to the figure of Boris holed up in a cupboard – hey, at least it wasn't a fridge this time – looking more of a slob than usual. Hair all over the place, eyes a bit bloodshot and a suit that had been thrown on at the last minute. It may have been possible to make less of an effort for one of the most important speeches of his career, but only if he had been sprawled on a wine-stained sofa.

Right chaps and chapesses, Boris barked with ersatz chumminess, the trademark smirk etched on to his face as his left arm waved up and down uncontrollably. Let's get this over and done with. 'Pifflepafflewifflewaffle,' he said. This was a time of celebration for some, anxiety for others and relief for the rest. You can't help feeling that for Boris alone, Brexit is actually a combination of all three. Though anxiety mainly. He's not good on keeping his promises.

Boris muttered a few lazy platitudes about how he was the man to bring the country together. And if you didn't believe him, you could always buy one of his Boris-as-Britannia-themed 'sod off EU' tea towels from the Conservative Party website. A bargain at just £12. 'This is a new beginning,' he said. One of the few accurate statements he made. And one of the most terrifying, because even he has to admit he doesn't have a clue what comes next.

Typically, Johnson then lapsed into contradiction and jingoist bullshit. We had outgrown the EU, but we could still be really, really good friends with the EU27, provided we remembered not to tell them we think they are a waste of space. And Britain had the best possible future ahead of it. Because . . . because we did. We're Britain and we could do anything. All you had to do was believe. This might have been more convincing if his own expression hadn't been riddled with self-doubt.

Er . . . Um . . . That was about it. He didn't have anything else to say. And what he had said hadn't been worth saying. At least not with the lack of interest with which he had said it. At a time of a national identity crisis, the prime minister had gone missing in action. All he had really managed to convey was an indifferent 'fuck you'. A sentiment that would have been echoed back to him by half the country.

* * *

After the general election of December 2019, Boris Johnson had delayed the reshuffle and reappointed all the same ministers to the cabinet. Even Nicky Morgan, who had stood down as an MP to take up a seat in the Lords – her reward for her late conversion to the Brexit cause. This had led to the absurd sight of the secretary of state for culture being unable to attend her departmental questions in the Commons. The reshuffle proper was to take place after the UK had left the EU on 31 January. Though some couldn't help wondering if the reshuffle would be more the work of Dominic Cummings than Johnson.

Javid's self-worth wasn't part of the plan for Cummi— sorry, Johnson

13 FEBRUARY 2020

It hadn't been one of Boris Johnson's more restful nights. First the succession of text messages from Dominic Cummings telling him who to sack. Then the nudges in the ribs from Carrie telling him who to keep. To top it all, he was still racking his brains trying to remember who had paid for his £15,000 winter break to Mustique. How could he be expected to keep track of that level of detail? He was fairly sure Prince Andrew didn't remember who had paid for all of his holidays.

Boris had dragged his heels before heading over to the Commons in the morning. He hated any form of confrontation and had hoped to get the tricky bits of the reshuffle done by text. Hell, it was the way he had ended all his affairs. And what was good for a lover was more than good enough for a mere cabinet minister. But Dom had insisted there was a protocol to be observed – 'Try to enjoy their pain' – and such matters were best done face to face.

First in was Julian Smith. The Northern Ireland secretary clearly had to go. You couldn't have a minister actually making a success of his job and getting better headlines. Geoffrey Cox was also a goner. The attorney general may have backed him for leader and gone along with the prorogation fiasco, but he was still far too outspoken and independent. Also, people tended to like him. Boris couldn't be having that. He couldn't wait to see Cox's face when he found out he was being replaced by Suella Braverman, one of the dimmest of all Tory MPs.

As for the others . . . Well, Andrea Leadsom was hopeless and talked too much. He hated opinionated women. Theresa Villiers was so forgettably ineffective he couldn't even remember who had appointed her to cabinet just six months previously. Esther McVey had just been collateral damage. 'It's nothing personal,' he had told her. Obviously, she had never achieved anything other than to increase homelessness, but that wasn't the point. If success was the benchmark, then almost everyone would have to go. It was just that there had been 10 housing ministers in 10 years, and her time was up.

The dirty business over, Boris sloped back to No. 10 to get on with the fun stuff. Dominic Raab and Priti Patel were shoo-ins. Raab could carry on doing what he was told, and it didn't matter that Nazanin Zaghari-Ratcliffe was banged up. Priti was a natural. It wasn't often you could find a home secretary who was both vicious and stupid. The ideal combo.

And though he'd teased Matt Hancock about being given the sack – who could resist that look of abject terror and insecurity? – it was useful to have a health secretary who was gullible enough to believe that 40 new hospitals were going to be built. 'Thank you, thank you,' Needy Matt had said on the way out. 'I love you, Daddy.'

Sajid Javid had proved rather more problematic. Boris had been certain that once he'd told him he could keep his job, so long as he was prepared to ditch all his staff and advisers and do whatever Dom said, then the CHINO – chancellor in name only – would roll over. After all, he'd pretty much done what he'd been told up till now by writing cheques for every scheme Boris had come up with. He hadn't even blinked at the idiotic fantasy bridge between Scotland and Northern Ireland. And he had happily laughed along when Boris had described Muslim women as letterboxes. But, seemingly out of nowhere, Javid had discovered some self-respect.

This hadn't been part of the plan. Boris had never encountered anyone with self-worth before. Least of all himself. Gaping wounds of shame masquerading as massive narcissistic egos, yes. But genuine self-worth, never. 'Are you sure, Saj?' he had pleaded. 'If you say no, then it's going to make it look as if I don't know what I'm doing.' Javid had merely shrugged and walked out.

At which point Dom had burst in. 'Every cloud and all that,' he had said. 'Don't forget, the point of the reshuffle is to settle scores, render every department effectively anodyne, settle scores, appoint figurehead cabinet ministers, settle scores and make me the most powerful person in the country.'

'Don't you mean me?' Boris had asked.

'Er . . . no. Now, where was I? Ah, yes. Let's get Rishi Sunak in instead. It would be a brilliant piece of levelling-up. Replacing a multimillionaire from Deutsche Bank with a multimillionaire from Goldman Sachs. Classic Me!'

Minutes later, Sunak found himself inside No. 10.

'Just one question,' said Dom, who by now had taken charge of the conversation. 'Are you a yes-man, Rishi?'

'Yes.'

'Great. You're chancellor.'

'Um,' whispered Sunak. 'I'm just not sure if I can write a budget from scratch in under a month.'

'Don't worry your pretty little head,' snapped Dom. 'I will be doing that.' This was his moment of triumph. He would be the first unelected chancellor to deliver a budget in the country's history. One in the eye for the unelected bureaucrats in Brussels. Take back control. Classic Dom.

After that, things had rather quietened down. Boris had had to concede that maybe Jacob Rees-Mogg did have a point about Grenfell residents being too stupid to save themselves, so he'd kept him on as leader of the house.

And Liz Truss had somehow survived the cull. Though only because he hadn't been able to find a phone number for Lynne Truss.

Best of all, he'd even been able to find a job for Stephen Barclay in the Treasury. Who cared if Nice Guy Steve didn't know anything about money? He'd never known anything about Brexit either. Ignorance was his greatest asset. The new mantra for the 'People's Government'.

Priti Patel's ineptitude is exactly what Boris admires in her

24 FEBRUARY 2020

It's not always a great look for a prime minister to have to publicly restate his confidence in his home secretary just a matter of days after reappointing her to the job. A bit like a football club chairman offering his full support to the manager just days before sacking him. But for once in his life Boris Johnson has been entirely genuine. Hard to believe, I know, from someone for whom dishonesty is a way of life, but true nonetheless.

Boris really, really does value Priti Patel. He doesn't care if she bullies her staff a bit. He cares even less if intelligence officials don't entirely trust her on matters of national security. Because that's not the point of her. Just as the home secretary can never be too Brexity or dog-whistle right-wing, she can also never be too stupid or incompetent. These are the qualities Boris most admires, having gone to some trouble to eliminate every cabinet minister who showed the slightest sign of having any independence of thought. Or even of having a mind at all. Priti Patel's sole purpose in government is to be Priti Vacant.

In her statement to the Commons on her new points-based immigration system, Patel was at pains to live down to expectations. If there were a points-based tally for a home secretary, then it's a racing certainty Priti would never have got the job. After all, this is the woman who responded to a terrorist incident by declaring war on counter-terrorism. On three occasions. She has turned her lack of ability into a piece of performance art.

What she does have, though, is the effortless self-confidence of someone who doesn't have a clue just how dim she is. She makes no effort to disguise her ignorance. Rather, she revels in it. And as she ran through the proposals the government had announced during recess the previous week, her smirk and swagger became steadily more pronounced. The country was wanting this, the country was loving this and the country was getting it.

For reasons that weren't entirely clear, Diane Abbott chose to sit this one out on the Labour front bench and let her junior shadow home office minister, Bell Ribeiro-Addy, point out some of the new system's more obvious flaws. That it failed to distinguish between low-paid and low-skilled work. That it would leave huge staff shortages in many sectors. That it presumed the reason most Brits weren't already doing these jobs was because immigrants had stolen them off them. Rather than that they just didn't fancy doing them.

Patel sighed ostentatiously and insisted that Ribeiro-Addy was just too stupid to have understood the proposals properly. Pots and kettles. At which point, Jeremy Corbyn intervened to say things might work a little better if the home secretary was a little less condescending. Priti merely replied that she too required courtesy and patience. Again, pots and kettles. The irony meter was now off the scale. Not even her friends have known her to be patient and courteous.

Most ministers might have a sneaking suspicion they are heading off the rails when the first four Conservative MPs to stand up to praise their intelligence and attention to detail are the notorious screwballs Iain Duncan Smith, David Davis, Owen Paterson and John Redwood. But Priti was in her element. Her *coup de grâce* was her insistence that the British people had voted for massive staff shortages in the NHS and social care. And if people were determined to die or grow old in squalor, then she was proud to be delivering on the will of the people. Back in No. 10, Boris could only applaud. This was the Priti he knew and loved so much.

Exit one brainless cabinet minister. Enter another. The environment secretary, George Eustice – Useless Eustice to his admirers – was at the dispatch box to explain why the government had done so little about the floods. Eustice's main observations were that it had rained much more than expected and that really most people had no one to blame but themselves for buying homes that had been built on vulnerable flood plains.

Labour's Luke Pollard expressed his pity for Eustice – it wasn't his fault that he wasn't very good at his job – and wondered instead why the prime minister had gone missing in action and had chosen to put his feet up at the nation's expense in the grace-and-favour mansion in Kent. Useless was outraged on his master's behalf. Boris had never pretended to be anything other than a bit lazy, and it was going to take a great deal more than a few damp patches to get him out of bed.

'Look,' said Eustice, trying to convince himself as much as everyone else. Boris had been to visit some flood victims in November, and if he were to make another visit, it would only encourage more people to flood their homes. Besides, the prime minister wasn't the sort of showman who thrived on attention and media opportunities; he was the master of dialectics. The details man who got things done precisely by failing to grasp the details. Not waving but drowning.

* * *

While the Conservatives tried to work out if they really did have a plan for Brexit after all, the Labour leadership campaign was well under way. Keir Starmer was the firm favourite; Rebecca Long-Bailey was considered by many Labour MPs to be too much the Jeremy Corbyn continuity candidate – a prospect not even die-hard Corbynistas could bring themselves to enthuse over, given the election wipeout – while Lisa Nandy was widely thought to be too inexperienced. Meanwhile, the first cases of Covid-19 were beginning to appear in the UK. By 1 March, 35 had been recorded in the country.

Boris fails to convince with sanitised take on coronavirus

3 MARCH 2020

And . . . breathe. Though not too deeply. And certainly not all over anybody else. After more than six weeks of mooching around No. 10 hoping the pangolins would deal with the coronavirus on their own, Boris Johnson finally broke off from his sabbatical to ease widespread concerns about a global pandemic with an emergency press conference. Don't panic! Don't panic!

There were no face masks or breathing equipment stashed in the corner of the state room. Just hand sanitiser at the front door on the way in. This was Downing Street in full 'Keep Calm and Carry On' mode. As Boris walked into the room, flanked by chief medical officer

Chris Whitty and chief scientific adviser Patrick Vallance, his trademark smirk was replaced by the serious face. It wasn't altogether convincing – it never is – but it was the best he could do. When you're trying to find the right words to tell several hundred thousand people they might die, it's probably best not to look too chipper. Don't panic! Don't panic!

Boris began by outlining the government's four-part strategy. Contain, delay, research and mitigate. He forgot to mention the fifth strand of 'doing almost nothing', which had been the plan up until the previous weekend. Everything was probably going to be more or less OK for most people, he continued, though for some people it would undoubtedly not be. Which was just one of those things. But try not to worry, as the NHS, already severely overstretched and underfunded, was uniquely placed to cope with an extra 2 million patients. Don't panic! Don't panic!

'The best thing you can do', Boris said, 'is to wash your hands with soap and hot water while singing "Happy Birthday" twice.' Mostly as an aspiration that you survive until your next one. Still, at least here he was on relatively strong ground. Because if there's one thing Boris knows something about, it's washing his hands. Over the years he's washed his hands of almost everything: family, children, friends, colleagues, morals, scruples. Pontius Boris.

Having listened in silence as the prime minister tried to minimise the situation, Whitty and Vallance were left to deliver a cold dose of reality. No one could say for certain just how bad things were going to get. But it would be at least another six months before we were out of the woods, and in a worst-case scenario, 80% of the country could catch the virus, with a mortality rate of about 1%. The young would probably be fine. The old, not so much. Bring out your dead! It would also be handy if the UK could work closely with neighbouring countries. If only there was a union of European countries of which we could be a part . . .

It rapidly became clear that the government's emergency plan was actually remarkably thin. Something that had been hastily cobbled together over a couple of days and didn't really stand up to close examination. There was nothing on what role the army might have to play, how health and social care workers could be protected, which hospital procedures would have to be delayed and what financial provision would be made for workers in the gig economy who weren't covered by employment law. It was all just a bit hit-and-hope. Don't panic! Don't panic!

The longer the press conference went on, the more uncomfortable the prime minister looked. Boris is essentially a good-time guy with a penchant for the glib one-liner. He hates being the bearer of bad news. He hates even more the idea that people might hold him responsible for the decisions that could cost lives. He just wants to keep things light and breezy. One of the things he had most liked about Brexit was that at least no one was that likely to die from it. Or not so anyone would notice. Now it was all getting just a bit too real.

Boris tried to cheer people up a bit. The good news was that if the coronavirus really did get everywhere, there would be no need for isolation units or preventing overseas travel. Though it might be an idea to visit only those countries with better health care than our own. There again, the shiny new blue passport did guarantee immunity from Covid-19 and all other foreign illnesses, so all was not entirely lost.

'We should all basically just go about our normal daily lives,' he said hopefully. Before telling the entire nation he had spent the last few days shaking hands with as many people who had contracted the coronavirus as possible. Whitty and Vallance perked up. They had at last tracked down 'Patient Zero'. The prime minister was the UK's own super-spreader. The man who had broken all the rules he was telling everyone else to observe.

As the pair walked away from the podium, they quietly advised Boris that a spell of self-isolation might do him and the country no end of good. Besides, it wasn't as if anyone would know the difference. After all, he was the first person on record to have started his paternity leave four months before his child was born.

An hour later, Matt Hancock delivered much the same message in a statement to the Commons. Weirdly, though, he sounded rather more convincing in saying he didn't know what he was doing than the prime minister had. When a 12-year-old Tigger is the one with gravitas, then it really is time to panic. Don't panic! Don't panic!

As Chris Whitty provides a dose of reality, Boris is just an annoying distraction

5 MARCH 2020

What a difference a week makes. For several years now, we've got used to being told that experts are a waste of space. Doomsters and gloomsters who trade in telling you things you don't want to hear. What was needed was a good, honest dose of mindless optimism to talk the country up. Want to believe that Brexit will be a brilliant success and there's an oven-ready deal to take us to the promised land? Then the Tories had just the government for you.

But now we're heading for several months of a coronavirus pandemic, the UK wants rather more than a prime minister who lies about building 40 new hospitals and a 12-year-old Tigger of a health secretary whose main contribution has been to replace his *Blue Peter* sticker with an NHS badge. Even Boris Johnson, the narcissist's narcissist who can't imagine a world without him at its centre, has had to bow to the inevitable and take advice from people who know what they are talking about. For a while at least, the geeks have inherited the Earth.

And the geek-in-chief, whom everyone now regards as the country's de facto prime minister, is Chris Whitty, England's chief medical officer. There's no one who wouldn't rather listen to a few minutes of Whitty than half an hour of Boris's bullshit. Temporarily at least, Boris has become a near irrelevance. An annoying distraction. Whitty first captured the nation's minds during Tuesday's Downing Street press conference, during which Boris's main contribution had been to make jokes and offer unscientific, cheery reassurances – reality has never been his strong point – and now he was back before the health select committee to provide rather more detail about the coronavirus crisis over the best part of two hours.

Whitty's only real downside is that he looks unfortunately like Chris Grayling. They could almost be brothers. But there the similarity ends. The moment Whitty opens his mouth, the words flow with liquid intelligence. His command of his subject and his ability to communicate that knowledge is near total. This is not a man whose solution to the pandemic would be to award a £13 million contract for hospital ships to a company with no ships.

There's something very weird about the choice of Jeremy Hunt as the health committee's chair. Rather like putting the chief suspect in charge of a murder investigation. The man who, as former health secretary, did more to screw up the NHS with endless cuts to provision and services is now responsible for finding out why the NHS is in such a mess and holding the culprits responsible. I'd imagine we're going to see Jeremy Hunt asking Jeremy Hunt some very awkward questions over the coming years.

That was something for another day, however – and if Whitty was as bemused as the rest of us to find a rather sweaty, twitchy and jacketless Hunt in charge of proceedings, he was too polite to let on. Rather, he merely restated the facts as he knew them. We had now moved on from the 'pretending nothing was happening and hoping it would go away' phase, which had been the government's plan before he had been brought onboard, and into delay mode. The idea being that the worst of the pandemic could be spread out over a matter of months to ease the pressure on public services.

Whitty never tried to soft-soap or minimise the situation. In a worst-case scenario, 80% of the country could get the virus, the mortality rate could reach 1%, with the elderly and those with pre-existing medical conditions most at risk, and there would be no chance of the NHS having enough beds. And though his attempts at reassurance – 'most people over 80 will live' – didn't sound particularly reassuring, there was something undeniably refreshing about his honesty and directness. Here was a man willing to treat the country as adults, and who didn't feel the need to lie about the severity of the situation.

Sadly, this isn't an attitude likely to catch on in government, as Boris was only too happy to demonstrate during a simultaneous appearance on ITV's *This Morning* with Holly Willoughby and Philip Schofield. Even when he strives for authenticity, he can't help being shifty. It's as though something within him can't survive contact with reality. He doesn't want to publish regular updates on the spread of the virus, not because the public can't handle the information, but because he can't. He just wants the crisis to be over and for people to get on with their lives; the anxiety and experience of going through it is anathema to him.

The dishonesty continued when the conversation turned to floods and to Priti Patel. After saying that he didn't want to interrupt the emergency services – though he was happy to let junior ministers do so and had been quick to do so himself during the election campaign – he went on to defend his home secretary and implied that the bullying inquiry would be a stitch-up because Priti was doing such a great job. A bit of bullying was healthy collateral damage. 'I hate bullies,' he said. Which is why he has Classic Dom as his chief of staff. The only bully one suspects he really hates is himself. His self-loathing is manifest in numerous displacement activities.

The one really jaw-dropping moment came when he was asked if he would change his baby's nappies. For almost every dad, this is a no-brainer, the very minimal level of care you would afford a child you had brought into the world. He was eventually shamed into saying, 'Yes, I expect so,' but it was clear Boris had no real intention of doing even this. Carrie must have watched in despair. She was going to be on her own with this one. There was little comfort for the rest of us either. If he treats his own family with such indifference, just imagine how he really feels about us. Just inconvenient satellites orbiting his world.

Later in the morning, Michel Barnier was left to give a solo press conference after the first round of the Brexit trade negotiations. The UK's David Frost couldn't be bothered to show up as he was desperate to get the hell out of Brussels and have a patriotic English breakfast. Barnier sighed heavily. The UK still didn't really have a clue just how complicated the negotiations were; it imagined that turning up and shouting, 'We're British!' would work wonders, he said. Much like our first response to the coronavirus. The thought occurred that if we also replaced Frost with Whitty, a trade deal would be a lot more likely.

Sunak's wholesale spaffing sends Tories into rapture

11 MARCH 2020

Some things are more important than the coronavirus. You'd have thought that once the junior health minister, Nadine Dorries, had announced she had caught it, some members of the government – Boris Johnson and Matt

Hancock among them – might have chosen to self-isolate. For everyone else's safety as much as their own. Other workplaces have shut down for less.

But this was Rishi Sunak's Big Day Out. A chance for the 16-year-old school prefect doubling as chancellor to splash the cash, to show that the 'People's Government' really did care for the lower orders, every bit as much as it did for the hedge funds that had bankrolled its election victory.

So the entire cabinet squeezed themselves along the front bench to cheer him on. Boris and Matt did their best to look really, really well – 'There's nothing wrong with us, guv' – while Psycho Dominic Raab discreetly coughed into his hands. No one passed him a tissue. Or a face mask. Rather, they tried to look as if they had not noticed, while slowly edging themselves away. Keep Calm and Carry On. Ish.

Sunak began by announcing £30 billion worth of measures to help the country get through the coronavirus epidemic, a serious amount of cash that rather suggested the government believes the situation is going to be a great deal worse than it has up till now been prepared to let on.

Everyone thought it best not to mention the fact that the NHS might be in a far better place if the Tories hadn't cut public services relentlessly for the past 10 years – the UK has fewer than half the intensive care beds of almost every other EU country. Or that people on zero-hours contracts were still vulnerable. Then we are in a new Year Zero where austerity never happened. The mere mention of George Osborne or Philip Hammond is enough to get you disappeared.

A wiser chancellor might have cut his losses after the coronavirus announcements. Just explained we were on the verge of a recession even before we had entered a crisis situation, so there were too many unknowns for any sane economist to make any credible future spending plans. Turned this into an emergency budget, with the promise of a follow-up when he had a clearer picture of what he was dealing with. There again, it might just be handy to have the coronavirus to blame when everything else goes tits up. You win some, you win some.

In any case, Rishi had another 45 minutes of *Noises Off* am-dram theatrics to get through. It's always the politicians with the least charm and charisma who feel obliged to go on the longest. He waved his arms about, told a couple of shit gags and indulged in a bit of call-and-response. 'We got Brexit done,' he squeaked. 'What else are we getting done?' 'Absolutely everything,' replied the Tory benches, reading from the Boris hymn sheet.

And in a way they were. Boris looked thrilled. Priapic, even. There's nothing he likes more than wholesale spaffing. After a while, even the Tory benches got into the swing of things. If this had been a Labour chancellor announcing the very same measures, the Conservative MPs would have been having a full-on Venezuelan

Marxist heart attack, but as it was their boy, they collapsed with multiple orgasms.

There was no end to Rishi's rabbits. Literally anything anyone had ever wanted, they could have. Hospitals? As many as you like. Trains, planes and automobiles? Go for it. Schools. Houses. Booze. Toys. Things. Stuff. There wasn't really a plan for any of this, but there sure was the cash. Not just for infrastructure projects, but also for day-to-day spending.

Sunak had no idea where any of the money was coming from – it sure as hell wasn't coming from his own pocket, as he intended to hang on to the fortune he'd made at Goldman Sachs – but the £600 health surcharge on every immigrant was a decent start. The right-wingers in his party would be salivating at the prospect of cracking down on a few foreigners. Who said this wasn't a budget for everyone? All the chancellor knew was that there was unlimited cash for everything. Apart from the things there wasn't cash for.

Just about the only Tory not to enjoy the occasion was Sajid Javid. The former chancellor looked thoroughly miserable throughout. This was Sunak stealing all his best lines. Even the ones about sticking to the fiscal rules, with a view to ignoring them at a later date. Rishi was on the up – a possible leader-in-waiting – while the Saj was going nowhere. Having an unexpected fit of conscience suddenly didn't look like such a good idea after all. He should have dumped his Spads and taken the glory.

As usual, Jeremy Corbyn replied for the opposition. Though he may as well not have bothered. He is already three months past his sell-by date, and no one in the Commons pays attention to a word he says. Even Corbyn appears to be bored by Corbyn. He made little effort to engage with anything Sunak had said and just read from his prepared script in a morose monotone.

There again, almost no one would care much about the budget by the end of the day. Within hours, the World Health Organization had declared the coronavirus to be a global pandemic and that many governments had been too slow to act. The UK being a possible case in point. *Sic transit gloria*, Rishi.

* * *

Despite nightly scenes on the TV news of hospitals in Italy struggling and failing to keep up with patients who were desperately ill with coronavirus, Boris Johnson continued to maintain a bullish attitude towards what, on 11 March, the World Health Organization had declared to be a global pandemic. Even though many UK holiday-makers had gone skiing in Italy during the February half-term break and it seemed inevitable to many scientists that what was happening in Italy now would be coming to the UK a fortnight later, Johnson and Dominic Cummings appeared to believe that the country could buck the global trend and beat the disease through herd immunity.

Already medical experts were crying out for a national lockdown, yet Johnson remained resolute that the UK could pull through without resorting to such draconian measures. So, on 11 March, Liverpool's Champions League fixture against Atlético Madrid went ahead at Anfield in front of a crowd of more than 45,000, including 3,000 who had made the trip from Spain. And a week later, on 18 March, the government allowed the Cheltenham horse-racing festival to be held, with more than 250,000 people rubbing shoulders with one another over the course of four days. Some might call this an act of negligence. Even when the number of cases reached 2,626 – with the death toll nudging past 100 and schools closed and exams cancelled – Boris refused to extend this to a full lockdown. It would later emerge that he had failed to attend five emergency COBRA meetings on the coronavirus.

However, while the government seemed to have been reduced to inertia by the crisis – its primary strategy seemed to be just to hope the coronavirus wouldn't be as deadly in the UK as it was elsewhere in the world – ordinary people were taking matters into their own hands by stockpiling food and other essentials. Notably, toilet paper. If we were all going to die, then at least we would do so with clean bottoms.

Boris Johnson unveils the lockdown that isn't quite a lockdown

23 MARCH 2020

This time there was no daily Downing Street press conference. Not even an ersatz 'People's' PMQs, with spoon-fed set-ups from Classic 'Let the old and the vulnerable die' Dom. Because in the last few days it's become clear Boris Johnson can't even prepare properly for a scheduled presser. Only the day before, he was telling everyone to keep two metres away from other people, when he was standing about a metre from the government's deputy chief medical officer. There was a time when he could just about manage two pages of A4 as a briefing paper. Now his concentration span can't even manage that.

So instead we got a six-minute televised address to the nation. Less chance of any unforced cock-ups and mixed messages that way. Telling people that they should try to keep their distance from one another but a day out to Skegness probably wouldn't hurt hadn't proved a spectacular success. So this time Boris tried to get serious. People should stay indoors, other than to exercise on their own or with family members, do essential shopping or go to work. It wasn't a total lockdown, but as good as.

The weird thing was, he was only telling most people something that they had already clocked long before him. It's been the country nudging the government into action, rather than the other way round. After all, these were the sensible measures many had already taken. On the coronavirus, the UK has had two months to learn from China what was coming and to make the necessary preparations.

And in that time Boris had managed to do next to nothing, apart from taking a week off over the half-term recess to pick a wedding date and argue over baby names. Still, he must be running out of possibilities by now. What was seemingly incomprehensible to Boris was that people really were now more interested in saving their own lives and those of others than being able to have a drink and a snout with Nigel Farage, Tim Wetherspoon and other members of the Brexit libertarian death cult.

Earlier in the day, during the debate on the coronavirus emergency contingencies bill in the Commons, Needy Matt Hancock, who's aged so much in the last few days he no longer needs to be ID'd in offies, had said: 'The government had made the most comprehensive public communications plans in history.' Presumably, he reckons recent messages to be the best since 'a leech a day keeps the doctor away'.

Still, better late than never. At least he had now heard of the police, a security enforcement service that had caught him by surprise the day before, though his hymn to the NHS felt hollow, coming from a government that had cut its resources significantly over the past 10 years.

But this was a last chance to head off a catastrophe on the Italian scale.

Boris looked thoroughly miserable as he was making the statement. Not just because of the gravity, but because even he couldn't escape the irony. Imagine a person who has built his entire career on being economical with the truth having to implore everyone to trust him. A prime minister who doesn't even look as if he could tell the truth to his reflection.

All his life Boris has wanted to be Churchill. Now he has met his Dunkirk, he realises he just can't do it. He doesn't have the leadership. He wants to be loved too much. Inside he's a ball of foetal need. The tousled hair is no longer endearing. Now it just looks shambolic. And the mind is as confused as the barnet. He's never come across a difficult decision he hasn't wanted to fudge. Marriages, affairs, Brexit. All compartmentalised away into a happy place where there are no consequences.

Being Draco the Lawmaker just doesn't sit well with him. Now the lives of thousands of people are at stake, and he can't bear the responsibility. He was only ever in it for the lols. He clasped his hands, as if trying to hold himself together, but his body is folding in on itself. Bags upon bags upon bags. Soon all that will be left is a pool of blubbery blob, its voice a faint echo of Rob Brydon's 'small man trapped in a box'. With the odd bit of Latin thrown in.

* * *

It was somehow inevitable that Boris Johnson and Matt Hancock would be among the first in Westminster to contract coronavirus. So with the prime minister and the health secretary out of action, it fell to other members of the cabinet – principally Dominic Raab, Michael Gove and Alok Sharma – to take what had become the daily ritual of the 5 p.m. Downing Street press conference. None of them looked entirely happy taking the stage . . . Meanwhile, with all hustings and campaign events having been cancelled for more than a month, Keir Starmer was quietly elected as the new Labour leader.

Queen praises the people, if not the government, and pulls off a tough gig

5 APRIL 2020

Now we know just how serious things are. The UK has just wheeled out its biggest gun. The Queen has only ever given an unscheduled TV address to the nation on four previous occasions, either when the nation or the royal family itself was under threat. And as sure as hell Her Majesty wasn't about to update us on Prince Andrew handing himself over to the FBI or Harry and Meghan's ongoing flat-hunting nightmare. This could only mean the country was in a coronavirus crisis.

Keeping one hand firmly clasped around her wrist and her body a safe distance from a lone BBC cameraman dressed in a hazmat suit – there's no shortage of personal protective equipment in Windsor Castle – the Queen, interspersed with footage of NHS workers and the wider general public, spoke to the country from her study. Wisely, she kept it short and sweet. This wasn't a Christmas message, when half the country would be pissed and the other half wouldn't be listening. Now every sentence would be picked over and every word would count.

The Queen began by acknowledging the challenges everyone was facing – death, financial hardship (some more than others, when it comes to the royal family) and separation – before going on to praise the selflessness of those in the NHS and other front-line emergency services. She then said how much she hoped people would maintain the self-sacrifice, self-discipline, compassion and sense of humour needed to defeat the illness.

On the hottest weekend of the year so far, this rang a little hollow, as most of the country appeared to have gone outdoors, with the sole purpose of snitching on any people they came across who weren't keeping the appropriate safe distance from one another. B&Q have had a massive run on tape measures in the past week. It won't be long before there's also a black market in tasers to take out sweaty joggers.

After a nod to the Commonwealth and the global nature of the pandemic – this wasn't the plucky Brits taking on the might of Nazi Germany single-handedly – the Queen mentioned a previous address she and Princess Margaret had made to the nation in 1940. Still, she could be forgiven the solipsism, as she had done her bit during the Second World War, having spent the latter years of the war driving military trucks. As yet there were no promises to turn any of the royal palaces into field hospitals or emergency supply depots, though she might be holding that in reserve for another day.

The Queen ended with a promise that better days would one day return, and in the meantime we should hold our nerve and do our best to be the generation of which future ones would be proud. We can but hope. She even came over a bit Vera Lynn, promising us, 'We'll meet again.' Only without the singing. Small mercies. Maybe next time. Given the circumstances, it had been more or less a pitch-perfect speech. After all, there's only a certain amount a head of state can say at times like these.

But one thing was notable by its absence. Although it's her job to be apolitical, there was no mention of the government's efforts or requests to follow official advice. Her Maj still hasn't forgotten how she was used, and made a fool of, by Boris Johnson over the prorogation and pointless Queen's Speech. In Boris, she doesn't trust. But then, who does?

The subtext was unmistakeable. If the country was to survive, it would do so through the collective resolve of its people, not through a government that had been slow to react and was still making promises it did not know it would be able to keep. And with that she faded out, after little less than four minutes.

Throughout, her face remained more or less expressionless – inscrutability to hide the pain – but she had done what was required. Simply by being there, she had shown she cared. She had provided the clear moral leadership that many politicians have failed to provide. For some people, nothing she could have said would have been enough, while others would have taken comfort. Most people probably wouldn't have cared much either way. But it was a necessary rite of passage. And a tough gig when underneath you're just as scared – if not more so, given her age – as everyone else. There's no disguising it: the Queen's a class act.

Ruffled Raab gives little clue of true state of prime minister's health

6 APRIL 2020

Just about the only reassuring thing to come out of the latest Downing Street press conference was that Dominic Raab does not yet have his hands on the nuclear button. Because in almost every other respect the foreign secretary appeared to be cosplaying Peter Sellers in *Dr Strangelove*. A man so clinically unstable he has yet to realise he is by far the most dangerous person in any room he enters.

The pathology manifests itself in different ways. Often Raab is a ball of barely repressed anger, the vein on this forehead throbbing metronomically as he tries to front out any tricky questions. Today, he was going for the more laid-back approach – the Mr Nice Guy who definitely had no guilty secrets. Unfortunately for him, he had more to hide than the usual collection of unsolved murders. Sooner or later, someone is going to have to have a quiet word with Dom and tell him he's crap at this gig. But then so is almost everyone else in the cabinet.

To be fair, Dom had been dealt a particularly bad hand. After the usual disclaimers about the government having done a generally brilliant job so far, the foreign secretary was rather obliged to give an update on the prime minister's health. Something he tried to mumble away as an afterthought. Boris Johnson was in top form, excellent spirits. In fact, he was having such a good time running the country from his bed in St Thomas' Hospital that he was planning to extend his stay to an extra night.

There was basically nothing wrong with Boris, was the message. He'd just dropped in at the hospital because he was getting a bit bored at home.

Understandably, no one was particularly convinced by Raab's 'He's in good spirits' explanation of the prime minister's health. After all, most people who have had even a mild version of the coronavirus have reported they were whacked out for the best part of a week and good for next to nothing. Yet here was Raab trying to persuade us that despite having a high temperature, a cough and breathing difficulties, Johnson was on top form and fit for anything. Being prime minister was actually a piece of piss that anyone could do from hospital. No big deal.

'He's in good spirits,' Raab repeated again, his eyes darting anxiously around the room. Mr Cool was now looking decidedly ruffled, and he inadvertently let slip the truth. The last time he had actually spoken to the prime minister was on Saturday, the day before Boris was admitted to hospital. So we were asked to accept that for the last two days he had been entirely out of the loop and that Boris had been running the show on his own. Not necessarily bad news for the country, but badly credible.

There was only one inescapable conclusion: that Boris doesn't rate either Raab or Michael Gove as suitable deputies to run the country in his absence and reckons that he could probably still do a better job than either of them from his hospital bed. It's a lack of trust with which most of the country has some sympathy.

Occasionally, Raab would desperately look to the newly recovered chief medical officer, Chris Whitty, and the Foreign Office deputy chief medical adviser, Angela McLean, for reassurance. Which they both refused to give. Though the nation was pleased to see him back, Whitty looked as if he would rather be elsewhere. Probably visiting his second home, like the Scottish chief medical officer. That way he would have to resign and wouldn't have to put himself through any more of these excruciating press conferences.

Long before the end, Raab had managed to muddle up even the most basic of messages. Last week, both Boris and the health secretary, Matt Hancock, had offered a glimmer of hope with a lockdown exit strategy, involving armbands and antibody tests. All that was now long forgotten, as Dom pointed to some slides that showed it was far too early to be making any of those kinds of predictions. We were going backwards fast.

A consistent display of hopelessness by the hopeless. A briefing that had served only to muddy the waters further, the Queen's call for national unity a distant memory. For what came through clearest was that no one in government really had a clue what was happening. Even the de facto prime minister wasn't being informed about the prime minister's condition.

Within hours, the mirage had disappeared, the press conference a total irrelevance. What Dom had or hadn't known was immaterial. During the afternoon, Boris's condition had worsened and he was being transferred to intensive care. Dom was now acting prime minister. All that anyone could do now was put their trust in the doctors and pray for the best. The crisis had just got significantly worse.

Leadership, Jim, but not as we know it with Captain Raab on bridge

7 APRIL 2020

It's now all down to a matter of trust. Last June, the Conservative Party decided it didn't rate Dominic Raab highly enough for him to even make the last five in the leadership contest. Imagine the humiliation of being considered to have less credibility than Michael Gove.

Yet now, with Boris Johnson in intensive care, Raab is the interim leader of the country, at a time of national emergency. 'You've got to ask yourself one question: do I feel lucky? Well, do ya, punk?' The answer for most of us is a resounding 'no'. We don't feel in the slightest bit lucky, thank you.

Neither, it seems, does Raab. The gap between vaulting ambition and practical reality has never seemed so wide. When he looks in the mirror, Dom no longer sees the decisive man of action he has always imagined himself to be. Rather, he just gazes at uncertainty and hesitancy.

The crown weighs far more heavily than he had ever anticipated. He can't even trust himself these days. The day before, he had insisted Boris was on top form and running the country from his hospital bed. Just three hours later, we were told the prime minister had been moved to intensive care.

It's hard to come back from that. Either the foreign secretary had been kept out of the loop about Boris's state of health or he had lied to the country. Neither of which was a good look for the man whose prime responsibility was to bring a sense of reassurance and stability to a country worried about the health of its leader.

Boris might not be everyone's idea of a national daddy, but he's the only daddy we've got, and no one wants to lose their dad. It's as primal and terrifying as that. The country hasn't felt this anxious and unsettled in decades.

Raab didn't look quite as sweaty and edgy on Tuesday as he had the day before; instead, the panic resided entirely in his eyes, which darted this way and that, avoiding direct contact with everyone. He started by getting to the question everyone wanted answered. The prime minister had been stable overnight, was receiving the best care and had needed no invasive ventilation. Good news.

'I'm confident he'll pull through,' he said. 'He's a fighter.' Cue a collective groan of despair. We were back in the mythology of plucky Brits single-handedly taking on the Hun. Fighting the coronavirus on the beaches and in the hedgerows.

We're not in a war. We're in a pandemic. The two things are totally different. And the many thousands who have already died from the disease did not do so because they were too weak or didn't fight hard enough. They died because they were too ill to live and there was nothing the doctors could do to save them.

46

The foreign secretary was no more convincing on who actually was running the country in Boris's absence. 'Government has always worked on collective responsibility,' he said casually.

Er, yes. Except the buck has always stopped with the prime minister. Now it seemed the buck stopped nowhere. All that was happening was that the entire cabinet was gathering round a crystal ball, while trying to channel the inner spirit of Boris.

And what was coming back was presumably total gibberish, as it's been well documented that in the week Boris was in isolation in Downing Street, the entire cabinet was squabbling like rats in a sack. Some have never even left the sack. Despite being home secretary, Priti Patel has never been allowed anywhere near a No. 10 press briefing. Small mercies, I suppose.

In the meantime, the Govester doesn't even trust Dom to make the coffee at cabinet meetings. God knows what would happen if there was another serious emergency, such as floods or a terrorist attack. The entire cabinet would be briefing against each other, with each person having a different idea of what Boris would really have wanted. Presumably, Mikey and Dom have already arm-wrestled one another for possession of the nuclear button. It's leadership, Jim, but not as we know it.

Nor did persistent questioning from the media about who was really in charge result in any more clarity. Everyone was just getting on and doing what Boris would have wanted, even though the circumstances might since have changed. All that did become clear was that Raab's idea of collective responsibility was every man and woman for themselves. Asked about the government's commitment to 100,000 tests by the end of the month, Dom casually threw Matt Hancock, the health secretary, under the wheels of a bus. Nothing to do with me, guv. Ask Tigger.

The only person to really level with the country was the chief medical officer for England, Chris Whitty. Thank goodness, he's back. After the chief scientific adviser, Patrick Vallance, had observed that the UK's death rates were broadly in line with those of Italy, Spain and France, Whitty alone dared to comment on why Germany's might be so much lower.

Testing, testing, testing. The Germans had taken the coronavirus more seriously at a much earlier stage than other countries and had planned accordingly. The UK was paying the price for its government having been too slow to act.

There was one adult in Downing Street, then. Just a shame he's not in the cabinet. Still, perhaps after Wednesday morning's fantasy football 'What would Boris do next?' cabinet meeting, one minister will be available to tell us who is really running the country while the prime minister recovers in hospital.

* * *

When the pandemic started, 99-year-old Captain Tom Moore decided to try and raise a few quid for the NHS by walking around his garden. Captain Tom captured the mood of the nation: while the ex-soldier found himself raising millions of pounds rather than the few hundred he had modestly expected, every Thursday evening at 8 p.m. the rest of country started a routine of going out on their doorsteps and clapping in gratitude for the NHS and care home staff. It sounds mawkish but was in fact extremely moving, a time when the public could briefly leave their homes and come together to thank those who were doing a great deal more than the government to fight the pandemic.

Hancock's shiny badge? Emblem of a scamper into Tigger mode

15 APRIL 2020

Cometh the hour, cometh the man. Or perhaps not. Matt Hancock had been expected to give the previous day's Downing Street press briefing but got pulled in favour of Rishi Sunak, following the publication of the Office for Budget Responsibility's report suggesting GDP was set to tank by 35% over the next three months. So you might have thought the health secretary would have used the extra 24 hours to fine-tune his announcements on social care.

Not so much. Over the past few weeks, Hancock has been one of the few cabinet ministers to look even vaguely competent, but today he let his department down, he let his country down, but worst of all he let himself down. And there's nothing worse than a Tigger who lets a Tigger down. The best he can do now is go home to watch a replay of his press conference and cry himself to sleep.

Hancock began by praising 99-year-old Captain Tom Moore for raising £7 million for the NHS by walking round his garden. As well he might. For that £7 million represents roughly the sum of what the Conservative government has taken out of the NHS each day over the past 10 years or so. Certainly, the legendary Chris Grayling has managed to waste twice that in a single visit to the dispatch box in the Commons.

Thereafter it was all downhill. I am here to tell you the next steps in our social care package, Tigger bounced. Which was news to everyone, as up till now even the first baby steps had been kept a closely guarded secret.

When Boris Johnson became prime minister, he assured the country he had a social care package ready and waiting to go. To go precisely nowhere, as ever since we've heard precisely zilch. *Nada*. Social care for the elderly still appeared to be the government's lowest priority, even during a coronavirus pandemic that dispro-portionately affected old people.

So here was the deal. More workers and care home res-idents would be getting tested, and there would definitely be more personal protection equipment available. Though starting from a baseline of near zero, this wasn't quite the earth-shattering announcement that Hancock had led everyone to expect.

But luckily, Tigger was planning on saving the best till last. Because he knew that what social care workers really wanted wasn't testing, PPE, more money or a home secretary who dismissed them all as low-skilled; it was a shiny new green badge saying 'CARE', which he was proud to model.

A badge. A sodding badge. Even the writers of the TV series *The Thick of It* wouldn't have dared come up with something as crass as this. Especially as it was a badge that had already been launched a year previously, to the general indifference of everyone in the care home sector.

This was Tigger's *Who Wants to Be a Millionaire?* moment. He was sorry that no social care workers had won the jackpot this week; the producers were withholding the £1 million top prize because they suspected cheating had taken place, as there had been a lot of background coughing during the recording of the show – but as a gesture of goodwill, and to make sure no one went home empty-handed, he would be giving every contestant a badge. And a Tigger cuddly toy.

Hard to believe, but the badges really were the high point of the entire 45-minute briefing. Hancock looked genuinely dismayed that the media weren't quite as wowed by them as he was – Fighting Corona, a Badge at a Time – and he rather went into meltdown during the question-and-answer session.

First, he made out that the reason testing levels had actually fallen in recent days was because NHS workers had been far too busy sunning themselves in the park during the Easter bank holiday weekend and couldn't be arsed to come in for a test. You can only imagine the conversations that must have been taking place all over the UK. 'Shall I go and get the test for which I've been begging for weeks? Or shall I just not bother and top up the tan?'

Hancock also appeared to be clueless as to why the government was seemingly unable to give even a hint of what criteria it would be using when considering a possible relaxation of the lockdown rules. There was no strategy to have a strategy. The best he could come up with was that different governments were at different stages of preparation, so it would be wrong to make any comparisons. The strong implication was that our government was still at the 'completely hopeless' stage of preparation, so we shouldn't be holding our breath for news any time soon. This is a decision that appears to be well above everyone's pay grade, including the prime minister's.

Even that wasn't the nadir. Matt can't go out to meet the press without having a plan of action involving numbers. Last time out he had a five-pillar plan, almost all of which were yet to happen. So why should anyone believe a word he said now?

Laura Hughes, of the *Financial Times*, gently pointed out that he had promised 25,000 daily tests by the middle of April, and we were still down in the 16,000s. Which made the 100,000 promise in two weeks' time look totally unrealistic.

Here Tigger lost the plot. It was all a big lie. A conspiracy. He had never said 25,000 tests by the middle of April. FAKE NEWS. He had said 25,000 by the end of April, which he had then increased to 100,000. So just wait and see. He believed he could fly. He believed he could touch the sky. Mystic Tigger. Unaccountably, Hughes was the only journalist not granted a supplementary question in which she could nail the inconsistencies in his memory. Instead, he bounced out of the room, kissing the badge in triumph. And there we all were thinking it was the bear who had the little brain.

A deflated Johnson struggles to muster his usual ebullience

27 APRIL 2020

Even the Messiah needs to ease himself back to work gently. So rather than hold a press conference in which he might be expected to face some tricky questions, Boris Johnson chose to mark his return with a quick statement outside a Downing Street decorated with children's tributes to the NHS, shortly after 9 a.m. in the morning.

Given that it's only two weeks since he came out of intensive care, this was unsurprisingly very much a Boris-lite appearance. Literally so, for he seemed to have lost weight, with his suit now being several sizes too large, his face washed out and tired and his hair in urgent need of a trim. Nor was there any of the familiar upbeat enthusiasm and ebullience to his speech. The references to Churchill all fell rather flat and his performance seemed to be geared towards reminding himself as much as the country that he was back in charge. On the upside, even an underpowered Boris is an improvement on Priti Patel or Grant Shapps.

He was here because he was here. That seemed to be the main thrust of what he had to say. He was grateful to the NHS, he was grateful to the public for by and large containing their impatience with lockdown – though the internal battle within his own cabinet on the timing of any relaxation in the guidance seems to have encouraged more people to make up their own rules – and we were making progress against the coronavirus mugger. Not exactly the best analogy to use, as the most sensible advice when faced with a bloke with a six-inch knife is to give him whatever he wants. In Boris World, a mugging is just a harmless duffing up by the Bash Street Kids.

'Many will be looking at our apparent success,' Boris continued. At which the only sound to be heard was of jaws hitting the pavement. To be fair, even he looked a

54

bit embarrassed at that line. So far, the UK has recorded more than 20,000 coronavirus deaths in hospital and possibly as many as that again at home and in care homes. Which would already be roughly the number of civilians who died during the Blitz, with the prospect of many thousands still to follow.

If that's a success, I'd hate to see what failure looks like. Or perhaps the prime minister regards it as a matter of honour to top the European mortality figures. Either way, most other countries will be looking at the UK as an object lesson in how not to handle a pandemic.

What followed was, in its way, just as startling. In claiming to have protected the NHS by flattening the rate of growth in infections, he completely forgot to mention his government's own negligence in failing to provide adequate supplies of personal protective equipment for NHS staff and care home workers. Nor did he offer any explanation or apology for his failure to take the coronavirus seriously right from the start of the pandemic, a decision that may have cost many thousands of lives. Nor was there any recognition that those countries which had implemented a rigorous 'test, track and trace' policy had achieved far more success in containing the coronavirus. Nor that his 250,000 daily testing target had always been bollocks. As so often, it was the subtext that provided by far the more informative meta-narrative.

By now, Boris was beginning to develop a hunted look in his eyes. His own brush with death has provided him with just a hint of conscience previously absent throughout his political career. The eyes are a window into a very troubled soul. He can sense the stench of battery chickens staying at home to roost.

He talked of transparency, when his government has done everything it can to keep Dominic Cummings's role in the SAGE meetings secret. He talked of bringing in opposition parties, though none would do so without first making clear that they would never have started from the current position. He talked of reaching the second phase, without saying how many phases he expected there to be. Mainly because he just doesn't know. Three? Four? Five? He's flying blind.

Just wittering on about enthusiasm and determination no longer cuts it. The situation has outgrown Boris's capacity for being serious. He knows he faces some tough choices in the next few weeks. A cabinet battle between the hawks who reckon tens of thousands more old people dying is a price worth paying to kick-start the economy and the doves who put the nation's health as their first priority is looming. With him stuck somewhere in the middle. And Boris has never been in politics to make enemies. He's Mr Fun Guy. All the tough decisions he has made have only ever been taken by accident, by default – the law of unintended consequences.

Now he really is going to have to take the tough calls that will define his legacy. The honeymoon period of his resurrection will be over in a matter of days. Then comes judgement day. Whatever he does, he risks losing the confidence of half the cabinet and half the country. And the tricky calls will keep on coming.

Over at the Brexit committee, Michael Gove had clearly taken far too many psychedelics, as he imagined the coronavirus could make a UK–EU deal far more likely. Hilary Benn, the committee chair, just looked bewildered. How can you possibly reach an outline of an agreement in two months, when no one has a clue what the global economy will be like in a year's time? Nor can you blame a botched Brexit deal on the coronavirus without first spelling out your negotiating objectives. Something the government has so far refused to do. Welcome to another week in the Fantasy Factory.

* * *

Carrie Symonds's pregnancy had been one of the worst-kept secrets in Westminster. For months, Boris Johnson had tried to keep the arrival of his – at a rough guess – sixth child out of the media spotlight. It had even been suggested that one of the reasons he had been so late to lock down the country was that he was preoccupied with sorting out his personal life, with an engagement and a baby shower to arrange. On 29 April, baby Wilfred was born.

Breathless Boris is left floundering as he faces foe he can't outbluster

30 APRIL 2020

Boris Johnson has every right to sound knackered. It's little more than a couple of weeks since he came out of intensive care, and his partner has just given birth to a baby boy. But sounding breathless before he had even gasped out his opening sentence at his first Downing Street press conference since falling ill with the coronavirus probably wasn't the commanding, reassuring presence he had hoped to convey.

The Boss may be back, but the man who longed to be the new Churchill isn't even the old Boris. The upbeat ebullience and jingoism no longer come naturally. He can still come out with the same words, but he can no longer bring even himself to believe them. For the first time in his life, there are signs of self-doubt. When he looks in the mirror, he now sees his reflection beginning to fragment. His persona, carefully constructed over 55 years to protect him from the pain of being himself, is falling apart. Yet still he can't quite access the humility that might go some way to healing himself.

Not that Boris didn't give it his best shot at papering over the cracks, but it cost him dear. By the end of the press conference he was just two pinprick, bloodshot eyes peeping out of an ashen-white face. If he really feels the need to get back to work so soon, then he can't have much faith in the rest of his cabinet. There again, that's one area where you can't really fault his judgement.

'I'm not going to minimise the lack of personal protective equipment or the failure to expedite testing,' he said. Before proceeding to do just that. The lack of PPE and adequate testing – today was the day we were supposed to have reached 100,000 daily tests – have been two of the leading factors in the UK's mortality rate, but according to Boris, the government hasn't put a foot wrong. The lack of an apology becomes more insulting by the day to the families of the nearly 27,000 people who have died. It appears that the only people in the entire country not to have heard of 2016's Exercise Cygnus, which highlighted the risks of a pandemic, are the entire government front bench.

Rejoice, rejoice. Sunlight was visible. We had avoided the worst-case scenario of 500,000 dead by burrowing under the alpine mountain. Boris appeared to have forgotten both that we were already well past the 20,000 'best-case result' of his chief scientific adviser, Patrick Vallance, and that – even allowing for statistical variations – the UK had a fatality rate significantly higher than that of Germany or South Korea, and might even have the worst record of any country in Europe.

The line that the government did the right things at the right time becomes ever more untenable. What can't be admitted is that Boris effectively took a 10-day holiday in March, at a time when he could have done more to protect the country. Seldom has so much been owed by so few to so many.

Boris then breezed on to the R rate – aka the reproduction rate. Here, satire nearly died. For as scientists struggle to pin down the UK's R rate to between 0.6 and 0.9, no one has the first idea of Boris's own reproduction rate. We know its current level is at least six – though even Boris doesn't appear to know if it's more – with every likelihood of adding to the score in the years ahead. If Boris were a virus, he would be deadly.

On and on he bumbled. We would have to wait until sometime next week for the government to make it clear it still had no real plan for ending lockdown. Things were definitely getting better, but no one had a clue how to ease things while ensuring R remained lower than 1. Even Vallance and England's chief medical officer, Chris Whitty, couldn't help Boris out with that one. The only certainty was more uncertainty.

The questions only revealed how little everyone really knew, as Boris had no clear answers to anything. He couldn't say anything on tourism to Cornwall – 'There will be more information later' – and his suggestion that people with mental health issues should call NHS helplines rang hollow, as successive Tory governments have cut mental health provision to a bare minimum. Even if you're really desperate, you're lucky to get an appointment inside six months these days. An embarrassed Whitty eventually had to intervene and point people in the direction of mental health charities if they needed urgent help.

Otherwise, there was just more of the same. The scientists urging caution, while Boris talked big about the economy bouncing back, avoiding the second peak and enforcing the wearing of face masks, which only a month ago he had said were a waste of time. But deep down, Boris knows he's met his match. Up till now, he's never found a situation in his life that he couldn't bluster his way out of. Now he's come up against a power greater than himself. Coronavirus is so far immune to almost everything. In a straight contest between coronavirus and bullshit, the coronavirus wins every time.

* * *

Almost on a daily basis, the news seemed to get worse and worse. On 5 May, the UK death toll became the highest in Europe, with over 32,000 people having lost their lives to Covid. Two days later, the Bank of England was predicting the worst recession on record, and it was announced that 400,000 PPE gowns imported from Turkey had been confirmed as useless. All the government could find to say in its defence was that it was 'following the science', to which most people quite naturally responded with scepticism. How come the UK was doing so much worse on testing than other countries? Why had we been so hopeless at closing our borders? Why had none of the lessons from 2016's Exercise Cygnus – the preparation for a pandemic – been taken on board? And this was all before we discovered that the government was handing out PPE contracts to Tory donors with no experience in delivering health equipment. Even so, on 10 May, Boris Johnson delivered his road map to recovery – less of a map and more of a magical mystery tour – with the new slogan 'Stay Alert'. As if there was anyone who wasn't worried about the coronavirus . . .

Smart suit, brushed hair. It was just Boris Johnson's speech that was a mess

11 MAY 2020

Stay alert. Watch out. There's a Boris about. All his life Boris Johnson has fantasised about being the next Winston Churchill, the nation's saviour. But 75 years after Churchill declared the end of the Second World War in Europe, all Boris could manage to do in his pre-recorded television statement – his minders don't trust him to do anything live – was divide the United Kingdom. The Scots, the Welsh and the Northern Irish had all managed to distance themselves from the prime minister's central message even before it had been broadcast. Forget

62

the Churchill tribute act; these days Boris couldn't even get a job as a Boris Johnson tribute act.

It was never intended to be this way. Boris was meant to be the man who could put a smile on the country's face; the man who would get Brexit done with blind optimism and a few white lies. But the coronavirus has put paid to all that. It's a virus that stubbornly resists any smooth talking about taking back control.

And deep down, Boris knows that he's well out of his depth – that he's simply not up to the job. You can see it in his eyes, which have shrivelled to puffy pinpricks. And he's lost the gift of language. At a time of crisis, a leader's speech is supposed to be a source of inspiration and reassurance. Somehow, all that Boris can manage to impart now is a sense of panic.

This time at least, Boris had made an effort. Smart suit, brushed hair. It was just the speech that was a mess. A more honest prime minister would have admitted that mistakes had been made in the handling of the crisis. But Boris is, deep down, a coward, a man who runs from the first hint of personal responsibility and has one eye already firmly on the public inquiry that will surely follow.

So what we got was more waffle about following the science and being grateful that even more people had not yet died. Why couldn't the 65 million survivors be a bit more grateful? Not a word on why other countries were coping with the virus so much better than us. It must be a huge relief to the families of those who have died that the government didn't choose to follow the South Korean science.

No one could have predicted the need for more personal protective equipment in care homes (unless they had actually read the Exercise Cygnus report that predicted just that). And we would soon be conducting hundreds of thousands of tests a day. Boris still clings to the belief that just by saying something, he can make it come true. Not only are we struggling to reach a target of just 100,000 a day without some creative accounting, we don't even have the resources to process the results in under 10 days.

Having got his excuses and disclaimers out of the way, Boris got down to the substance of his speech. Or rather the lack thereof. Meet the new messaging: same as the old messaging. Only even vaguer and more confusing. Not so much 15 minutes of TV fame as uncomfortably like watching someone have a breakdown in front of you. Rather than just to stay at home, Boris's new maxim was to 'Stay Alert'. Less a slogan, more like a piece of advice to himself, given all the times he has taken his eye off the ball over the past few months. Even the writers of *Dad's Army* wouldn't have let Captain Mainwaring embarrass himself like that. It was as if what was missing was some blackout curtains and taking down road signs in a bid to confuse and slow the progress of the coronavirus. The one war slogan that might have been more apt was:

'Careless talk costs lives.' Because few people's talk has been more careless than the prime minister's. He's a Zen master whose only objective is to get to the end of any one sentence, with no thought for the consequences for those that follow. For Boris, there is no past and no future. And, as things stand, not much of a present.

What was most striking was how little Boris had to say. His road map – or 'shape of a road map', as he called it, making it sound uncomfortably like a homeopathic memory of a map – to the future looked uncomfortably like one of the M25. There were five exciting colours of alertness and the promise of a Captain Marvel bio-science centre, but the bottom line was that it was still circular, with any number of still-to-be-determined exit points, keeping alive the very real possibility that we might find ourselves back at the start.

Much of it was just the same – often contradictory – advice. Social distancing, staying at home wherever possible, going to work wherever possible. How people were meant to get to work on public transport while staying two metres apart was not explained. He also gnomically stated that the reproduction rate had now come down far enough for us to test arrivals at airports in a month's time. Clearly, he's been spending too long talking to Priti Patel, who insists the UK has both too many and too few air passengers to make testing a viability. There would also be some easing of the lockdown by the end of June (apart from the bits that might come sooner). (Or later.) It was all just a bit of a ramble, with nothing on the one question many people wanted answered: at what stage might people be allowed to see their family and friends again?

'This is our plan,' Boris concluded, having forgotten he had just said he didn't really have a plan, other than to stay alert and keep buggering on – something the rest of the country is increasingly wishing Boris might personally reconsider. Remember those far-off days when you thought we had scraped the barrel with David Cameron and Theresa May?

Boris Johnson resorts to bluster under Starmer's cross-examination

13 MAY 2020

On Monday, Boris Johnson was singing the praises of 'good old-fashioned British common sense'. A higher order of common sense than French or German common sense, naturally. So it's unfortunate that this is the very quality he seems to singularly lack. Because you'd have thought the one thing Boris might have learned from his first time up against Keir Starmer at prime minister's questions last week was that it would be a help to come properly prepared.

But Boris has never done preparation for anything. It's not in his nature. Preparation is for girly swots. He is a *tabula rasa* who treats every day as a new beginning. One free from the consequences of any past actions. He is the macho blagger who has always been able to wing it, fuelled by a few gags and some hasty last-minute revision – something that might have been good enough, when backed up by a full chamber of braying Tory MPs, to see off Jeremy Corbyn, but which is proving hopelessly inadequate against a top QC in a near-silent courtroom. Things are now so bad that every time Boris opens his mouth, he only encourages the jury to convict him and the judge to increase his sentence.

It's also possible that Starmer has made the same mistake as many people in severely overestimating Boris's intelligence. That the long words and the Latin phrases simply cover up the fact that the prime minister isn't particularly bright; after all, it takes a very special type of cleverness to keep making the same mistakes over and over again. But then old habits die hard for the leader of the opposition too. He has learned from his time at the bar that there's no such thing as having too much evidence against a defendant, so he was taking nothing for granted by coming to the Commons somewhat over-prepared.

Give it time and Boris may well cut to the chase and just plead guilty in advance to save him the torture of answering six questions, but we're not there yet, so Starmer opened his folder and asked the court to consider Exhibit A. Care homes. Was it not true that the government had been far too slow to act in protecting the most vulnerable members of society? Absolutely not, Boris insisted. No country had done more to protect the elderly. What better protection could anyone get than being killed?

Hmm. That was weird, Starmer said, because in Exhibit B he had a surgeon, quoted in the *Daily Telegraph* – citing the newspaper that up till now had been only too happy to print any old rubbish the prime minister writes was a cruel twist of the knife – saying that the government hadn't changed its advice on releasing untested patients into care homes until mid-March.

That's just not true, Boris blustered, sounding guiltier by the second. Even though it was true. Though to accuse the prime minister of lying is to commit a philosophical category error. As Boris has no clue what advice his government has and hasn't given, he can't knowingly be untruthful. Nor, given his career track record, can he show any sign of being able to differentiate between truth and lies. Rather, he just recites the answer that he wants to be true and hopes to make it so by willpower alone. And to be fair, it's a tactic that's worked often enough in the past.

Starmer moved on to the Office for National Statistics' figures for deaths in care homes. Their report suggested there had been 18,000 excess deaths, yet the government was certain that only 8,000 of them had died of the coronavirus. So what did he think the other 10,000 had died of? Boris shrugged. It was a huge mystery. Perhaps some were dying of happiness. Or of over-exertion in the gym during lockdown. Or perhaps they were dying of disappointment that the UK still had not technically left the EU.

'I'm baffled,' said Starmer. Baffled is QC-speak for 'Now I've got you nailed, you filthy lying toerag.' Baffled that the government had stopped using the international death rate comparison at the Downing Street press conference, having done so continuously for the past seven weeks.

Boris blustered yet again. It turns out that a prime minister who was supposed to be such a great communicator can now barely talk in joined-up sentences. He has regressed to the pre-verbal stage. 'Um . . . er . . . ah,' he mumbled.

There was little left of the prime minister but a sodden mess by the time Keir had finished with him, though the SNP's Ian Blackford was happy to make a few ripples of his own in the pool of blubbery sweat previously known as Boris. All that Johnson could say in his defence was that his was a road map of consensus – the consensus being that he hadn't bothered to consult Scotland, Wales and Northern Ireland. It appears he was surprised to learn there were so many people in London who needed to use public transport.

In other times it might have been uplifting for the opposition benches to see the prime minister so comprehensively dismantled. But there was little cheering or sense of satisfaction, because in a time of crisis you rather hope the country would have a leader in whom you could

69

believe. Someone you could trust to make at least some of the right decisions. But we have Boris. Incompetent, unprepared, selfish, lazy, amoral and just not that bright. And no matter how many times Starmer batters him with an indefensible charge sheet at PMQs, Boris will remain prime minister for the duration.

* * *

There's sometimes a fine line between a government reacting nimbly to events and one that appears to be totally at sea. But right now, Boris Johnson was working overtime to make it abundantly clear that his government had chosen to come down on the side of complete cluelessness. On 20 May, Boris had been adamant that it was entirely right for overseas nationals to pay a £624 visa surcharge for the privilege of working in the NHS and social care sectors. Less than a day later, after significant pushback from all the opposition parties and some of his own MPs, Boris had a change of heart. Overseas nationals would be exempt.

Worse was to come, when the Guardian *and the* Daily Mirror *broke the sensational story that Dominic Cummings had broken lockdown regulations by driving from London to Durham when he, his wife and their child all suspected they had coronavirus. Even more damning, they had all been seen some 10 days later on an Easter trip to Barnard Castle. For most special advisers, breaking the rules in this way and damaging the government's pandemic messaging would have been a sackable offence. But Cummings was too powerful to sack. So what we saw was Boris and other ministers selling what was left of their souls to protect him. Classic Dom.*

No dignity, no future: Boris forsakes leadership to protect Cummings

24 MAY 2020

Look on the bright side: at least we've had it confirmed who is actually running the country these days. And it isn't the prime minister. Boris Johnson is no more than Dominic Cummings's sock puppet. A fairly shabby one at that. The reality is that without Classic Dom, there could be no Boris. All that Boris really amounts to is a parasitical ball of compromised ambition, fuelled by a viral overload of neediness and cowardice. There is no substance or dignity left within the prime minister. His only instinct is his own survival.

The equation was quite simple. If Dom was to be fired, then Boris would have to fire himself, because it is inconceivable that the ersatz prime minister didn't know the de facto prime minister had broken the lockdown rules by doing a runner to Durham. But just in case Boris had been in any doubt, Dom had arrived at Downing Street four hours before the daily coronavirus press conference to remind him who was boss. There were to be no sackings and no resignations. Not yet anyway. There may be in the days to come.

Not that Boris had actually wanted to front up the No. 10 briefing. It was just that every other cabinet minister had phoned in to say they were self-isolating in their second homes. Or in Robert Jenrick's case, his third home.

Right from the off, Boris looked rattled. The self-styled great communicator has lost the power of language and can now only talk in staccato bursts of incomprehensible Morse code. Even more disastrously, he is the populist politician who has lost track of the mood of the people. His survival skills have deserted him. The country is spitting blood at the arrogance of one rule for the elite and another for the rest, and Boris is totally oblivious.

Breathless and pasty-faced, his eyes still bloodshot after his talking-to by Dom, Boris leapt to his boss's defence. He hadn't been able to throw a protective ring around care homes, but he sure as hell was going to throw one round Cummings. Classic Dom had done nothing wrong at all. In fact, he had done what any father would do and drove to his second home. Mostly because he was so short of friends that he had no one within a 260-mile radius who could leave food parcels for his child. Oddly, that was one of the few statements that sounded vaguely convincing.

The rest of his opening remarks were incoherent drivel. Dom had driven the length of the country to escape the virus. Even though he was taking it with him in the car. It was as though Boris thought the virus could only travel at 50 mph, so if Dom drove at 70 mph up the M1, then he could outrun it.

Dom had had no alternative. Indeed, if the de facto prime minister had a fault, it was that he loved his family too much. All those single mothers and work-shy parents without second homes were basically heartless and uncaring for staying put and obeying the government advice on self-isolation. Dom: the man who loved too much.

Boris then wittered on a bit about schools – mysteriously, he seemed to forget the dualling of the A66 that Grant Shapps had been so desperate to talk about during the morning media round – but all the questions concentrated on how and how often Dom had chosen to arbitrarily break the rules. Here Boris started to get sweaty and petulant. He was standing by Dom, and that was that. He didn't have to give a credible reason because he was the World King who wrote all the rules.

Bizarrely, he even described Dom as responsible. Cummings won't be at all happy about that. His whole self-image is based upon him being the great anti-establishment disruptor, the person to whom rules don't apply. Not some establishment posh boy who toed the line at all times. God save the Queen! Her fascist regime.

Then Boris was unwittingly making sure that both he and Dom had no future. The press conference he had hoped would draw a line under Dom's midnight – no toilet or snack breaks – flits to his hideout merely served to ensure they would dominate the news agenda for weeks. Boris had had a chance to show genuine leadership and completely flunked it.

He refused to answer any questions about whether he knew Dom had done a runner – just imagine Boris working from Downing Street imagining his host body was holed up in north London – or when he discovered that Dom was in Durham. Not because he didn't know, but because he genuinely thought it didn't matter. Boris is a true believer in his own exceptionalism, a trait that he graciously extends to those who are close to him. He genuinely doesn't see a problem with not obeying a rule himself that he has asked the rest of the country to follow. So what if Dom and his family might have risked infecting a few dozen inconsequential little people? Sacrifice is what other, lesser people do. Nor was there even an attempt to answer the allegations about Dom's other alleged extracurricular outings to Barnard Castle or the bluebell woods.

In saving Dom – for the time being at least – Boris had tossed away the credibility of his own government. He has been stripped bare and exposed as not very bright, lacking in judgement and completely amoral. Within an hour, he had not only defended the indefensible, he had basically told the nation they were free to do as they pleased. If there is a second coronavirus peak, Boris will have even more blood on his hands. He'd even made Shapps's TV appearances look vaguely statesmanlike. That bad. At a time of national crisis, we have a prime minister who makes Henry Kissinger look worthy of a Nobel Peace Prize. Satire is now dead.

Regrets? St Dom had a few, but then again, too few to mention

25 MAY 2020

Classic Dom: Downing Street's very own Prince Andrew. Show how much respect you have for the public and the media by turning up 30 minutes late for your own gig. There again, start as you mean to go on. Because Dominic Cummings's press conference in the Downing Street Rose Garden was all about his own exceptionalism. How the rules applied differently to him than to the little people.

On Sunday we had Boris Johnson, the understudy prime minister, trying and failing to convince the country that there had been nothing untoward about Cummings's trip to Durham. A midnight flit that had been so normal that Downing Street had spent the best part of six weeks trying to cover it up.

Now we were to get the full story – or what approximated to it – from the person who is really running the country. And what we were treated to was an hour-long confused ramble that was disguised as the martyrdom of St Dom. A man who had only ever acted in the best interests of his family and the country. A man more sinned against than sinning.

'Hi there,' he said, when he eventually turned up after a half-hour row with his wife over whether he really needed to change out of his hoodie and put on a shirt. 'Sorry I'm late.'

He wasn't, of course. Dom is never sorry about anything, but that was the closest we were going to get to any form of apology for having driven 260 miles to Durham to self-isolate on his parents' estate, when the rest of the country were obeying the letter of the law, which he had helped write, by staying at home.

Much of what Dom had to say made little sense. His wife had initially been ill, but he had broken with his own health guidelines by going into work the following day. He had then decided to exploit a loophole involving young children that had never been intended to apply to families in his position and drive to Durham.

And no, he hadn't bothered to get any medical advice or tell Boris what he was planning on doing. Because he was the Special One – the real prime minister – so there was no need. Indeed, he might only have told Boris where he was a week later, and by then they were both so ill that they conveniently forgot about the conversation until the *Guardian* and the *Mirror* rudely reminded them.

That was just the start, though. His car had had a full tank of petrol – nice touch – and his son, who couldn't last a 30-minute drive to Barnard Castle without stopping for a pee, had proved iron-bladdered for the entire six-hour journey north. Once in Durham, both Dom and his wife Mary had been ill with coronavirus. They had broken lockdown only once by nipping out to the local hospital because their son was unwell, and had self-isolated for the full 14 days.

Then, on the 15th day, St Dom had risen again. And although he was still feeling shit, he felt ready to go back to London to start running the country again. There was just one small problem: his vision was playing up. So the obvious way to see if he was safe to drive was to pack his family into the car and make a 30-mile journey to Barnard Castle. Not quite sure if that's in the DVLA guidelines. There they had stopped and sat by the river for a bit – their entire conversation had been focused on the state of his eyesight – before heading off back to Durham for a walk in his private bluebell wood.

All this was said in a state of barely repressed anger. This statement was costing Dom dear. Classic Dom never explains and never apologises. And even though not a word of apology escaped his lips, you could sense that this whole exercise felt uncomfortably close to one. Just having to appear in front of journalists for whom he felt nothing but contempt and pretend to be Mr Polite Nice Guy was a humiliation he couldn't bear.

Once the questions started, the mask began to crack. He was just doing what anyone else would have done in the same exceptional circumstances. Except they hadn't been doing that. People in far more testing situations, without the comfort of a second home 260 miles away, had obeyed the guidelines. Because they were mugs. The proles who weren't able to think for themselves. If he had a fault, it was that he was just too loving and law-abiding a father. Regrets, he had a few. But then again, too few to mention.

Time and again he was asked to apologise, and every time he refused. Anything but that. Everything was totally above board, which is why he and his wife had both written stories in the *Spectator* that they knew to be misleading. Perhaps he and Mary had both been so delirious it had slipped their minds to point out they hadn't been in London.

Then he went full-on Trump. Everything that had been written about him was completely Fake News. Apart from everything in the *Guardian* and the *Mirror*, which he had as good as corroborated.

Had he thought of offering his resignation? A dismissive shrug. Who was he going to offer it to? Himself? There was no point in offering it to Boris, because why would you ask your understudy? Just remember who worked for whom here.

It ended in a stand-off. If Dom had imagined this press conference would clear the air, then he had misjudged the mood of the nation, just as he had by pleading for his

78

own exceptionalism. There was also a deep irony in that a man whose entire political reputation had been founded on the simplicity of his messaging was now pleading for his career on the basis that life was complicated. He even concluded by saying there was no point in answering some questions because the answers could be more confusing. So the journos could get lost.

There was to be no redemption for Laughing Boy. His presser may have satisfied a few of the Boris faithful, but the majority of the country could only see a man who had chosen to break the rules and had – worse still – put the nation's health at risk by effectively telling everyone they could interpret the rules however they wanted.

Not that Dom would have cared that much. What would have hurt the most was that he had been seen for who he really was. A man who can turn any hint of regret into a giant 'fuck you'.

Floundering Boris leaves no doubt: our PM is a showman out of his depth

27 MAY 2020

We've reached the point where the only way to understand the state the country is in is to realise that it has become a banana republic. A failed state run by a bad joke of a prime minister, who prioritises the job security of his elite advisers over the health of millions. A man who sees no need to be across the most basic points of government policy and is so inarticulate that he can't even start a sentence, let alone finish one.

It's normal for a prime minister to appear before the liaison committee – the supergroup of select committee chairs – at least three times a year. This was the first time Boris Johnson had bothered to turn up in more than 10 months. And you could see why. Even with Dominic Cummings sitting just off screen – Boris's eyes kept darting to the right, desperate for help – holding up placards with something approximating an answer, Johnson was lost for words. The great populist who doesn't even realise he has long since lost the support of the people. A mini-dictator surrounded by yes-men locked inside the No. 10 bunker.

What made this even more pathetic and desperate a spectacle was that Boris clearly believed he had prepared thoroughly. If he had, then his short-term memory is completely shot. It's more likely, though, that Boris's idea of preparation is just a quick 10-minute skim of a briefing note.

Boris is the supreme narcissist, the apogee of entitled arrogance, where other people are there only to serve his needs. A fragile ego, disguising an absence of any self-worth. What's more, you sense he knows it. That in the wee, wee hours he looks through a glass darkly and sees the blurred outlines of his limitations and failures.

The session started with questions from committee chair Bernard Jenkin, and Boris was clearly expecting friendly fire. Only to many people's surprise – possibly even his own – Bernie turned out to be no patsy. Instead, he went straight to the point. Why was there to be no cabinet secretary inquiry into Dominic Cummings's clear breach of the government's coronavirus guidelines?

'Um . . . er . . . well,' Boris blustered, looking frantically to Classic Dom for help. Up went the placard: 'It's time to move on.' 'Um . . . er . . . well . . . I think what the country wants is to move on,' he said.

What the opinion polls have clearly shown is that at least 70% of the country think that Laughing Boy is basically taking the piss – one rule for the elites, another for the little people. Only Boris somehow ignored that, believing that he knew what the people really thought better than they did. Who would have guessed that Boris would have subscribed to the Marxist idea of false consciousness?

Six times Boris insisted that the country wanted to move on. Something I'm sure the families of those who have died – not to mention the many thousands who could yet die as the prime minister trashed his own public health message to protect a chum – must have been delighted to hear.

Pete Wishart, Meg Hillier and Yvette Cooper all went in for the kill. Had Boris actually seen the evidence that Cummings had provided for his special and different

Covid-19 fortnight away on his father's estate? Boris nodded fiercely. He had. And the evidence was that it was Dom who was running the country, and he didn't have the power to sack him.

Nor could he explain the difference between deputy chief medical officer Jenny Harries's clear instructions to stay at home and the supine advice of several cabinet ministers, who had insisted that maybe having to look after your own child constituted exceptional circumstances. Boris's best guess was that maybe Harries hadn't been as clear as he would have liked her to have been, and he hoped that she would come on message in the near future. He ended the section on Cummings by insisting that all the stories that Dom had corroborated in his Rose Garden press conference were essentially false.

Things didn't improve when Jenkin moved on to other areas of the government's handling of the coronavirus. Boris had only the sketchiest idea of how the new track-and-trace system that was meant to come into operation the following day would work. A nation panicked. He even said he was forbidden from making any promises on dates for reaching government targets. Let that sink in. The prime minister is forbidden from making his own policy. If we had been in any doubt about who was running the country, we weren't any more.

Boris didn't even know the basics of how his own benefits system operated. This was Government 101, and the prime minister was still out of his depth. During the worst health crisis for a century, we are lions led by dead donkeys.

Boris Johnson sacrifices top scientific advisers on altar of Classic Dom

28 MAY 2020

Yesterday I wrote that the best way to understand the state the country is in was to consider it a banana republic. I'd meant it as a joke, but at the Downing Street press conference Boris Johnson went out of his way to prove me right. The UK's very own dictator might not have much of a reputation left to protect, but Chris Whitty and Patrick Vallance most certainly do.

Yet to save what now passes for his career, Boris went out of his way to trash the reputations of both the chief medical officer and the chief scientific adviser. Just as unbelievably, a plainly terrified Whitty and Vallance just stood there and took it. If either had a smidgeon of self-worth, both would have walked out once the questions began.

It seems that many people have been making simple category errors with Boris. They have assumed that Dominic Cummings's understudy has both intelligence and morality to compromise. That's why more than 70% of the country had said that Johnson should do the right thing and sack his special adviser for breaking the guidelines and undermining the government's public health message.

Yet the evidence all points to something more disturbing: that beyond an ability to recite the odd Latin phrase, Boris is actually quite dim. Worse still, he is totally amoral. So the very idea of him doing the right thing is a complete non-starter.

Right from the start of the briefing, Boris set out to gaslight the entire nation. Things were great. Improving rapidly. So he was now in a position to re-announce some easing of the lockdown measures that he had already announced during the previous week. Sure, it might be a bit of a risk, as the track-and-trace programme wouldn't be properly up and running till the end of June. But hey! The weather was nice, and everyone deserved a break. And he really appreciated the sacrifices that everyone had been making so that Dom and his family could have a well-earned day out at Barnard Castle.

Even Whitty and Vallance appeared slightly taken aback by Johnson's bullish optimism. Matt Hancock might have found it hysterically funny that the UK now had the worst death rate in the world during an interview with Kay Burley on Sky, but they both thought the situation was basically a bit shit and that we were a long way behind most other European countries.

It was when the questions started coming in that Boris went full psycho failed state. Given this was the first time that the CMO and CSA for England had been allowed out in public since Cummings's moonlight flit to Durham had come to public notice, most journalists were keen to know if Whitty and Vallance endorsed Classic Dom's course of action during the end of March and the first two weeks of April. But before either had a chance to speak, Boris effectively silenced them. They wouldn't be commenting on this, he said, before preventing Laura Kuenssberg from asking a follow-up question by muting her.

Almost every other journalist had similar questions. And each time Boris either ignored them or just repeated that Whitty and Vallance couldn't get involved in political issues. It's possible that both men had only agreed to stand alongside the Great Dictator on the proviso they were allowed to say nothing. If so, that was a huge mistake on their part, because reputations that had taken decades to build were shredded in a matter of minutes.

The whole point was that the scientific and the political have become entwined, not least because Laughing Boy had chosen to make it so. And the questions the scientists were being asked were matters of scientific judgement. Would they recommend doing what Classic Dom had done? Was that the public health message they wanted to put out to the country? Yet under a lot of pressure from Boris – you can add bullying to his character defects – they both played dumb. Better to have refused to prop up Boris than to have been used as mugs.

Whitty and Vallance weren't even allowed to answer the basic question of whether they would recommend a 50-mile round trip, with your child in the back of the car, as a good way of checking if your eyesight was fit for driving. That was about as straightforward a scientific 'yes' or 'no' question as you could get. But still they didn't dare say a word.

Other pressers have been tetchy and opaque, but this one had been a new low. Boris hadn't demeaned himself, because there's nothing left to demean. But he had demeaned his CMO and CSA, and he had demeaned the UK by treating its citizens with total contempt. In saving Dom, he has ruined what was left of his credibility. And all across the country, Tory MPs and Tory voters were beginning to ask themselves one simple question: ever get the feeling you've been had?

No hiding place for Boris at PMQs

3 JUNE 2020

You can sense the growing disbelief and anger. All his life Boris Johnson has been told that he is the Special One. A person for whom all rules are there to be broken. He is a man who has consistently managed to fail upwards. Sacked from one job for lying or incompetence, he has always effortlessly moved on to a better one. Friends, family and children have only ever been collateral damage in a ruthless pursuit of an entitled ambition.

Yet now there is no hiding place. Boris has achieved his narcissistic goal of becoming prime minister, and from here the only way is down. And it's a lonely place to be, because even he can't escape the fact that he's just not cut out for the top job. It's not just that it's too much like hard work and he is basically lazy; it's that he's not that good at it. Lame gags, bluster and Latin free association just don't cut it.

Put simply, Boris isn't as bright as he has come to believe he is. In fact, he's quite dim. And nowhere is this more evident than when he's up against Keir Starmer at prime minister's questions, in front of a near-empty chamber. During their first few outings, much was made of how Boris crumbled in the face of the Labour leader's forensic questioning. But now it's clear Johnson can't cope with any kind of questioning at all. Because even when Starmer isn't at his absolute sharpest, Boris begins to fall apart. It's as if he knows he's up against a man of greater intellect and morality, and his only defence is to lash out.

It doesn't help that Boris has become his own worst enemy. The charmer turned charmless. Mr Happy turned Mr Angry. It also doesn't help that even when his friends at the *Daily Telegraph* try to big him up with a story about how he was going to take direct control over the government's handling of the coronavirus, they only succeed in teeing up Starmer with his first free hit. Who had been in charge of the government during the past three months? Apart from Classic Dom, of course. Because we could all take that as read.

Boris immediately became defensive and snappy. He had always been in control. All that was changing was that now he would be in total control. Besides, he stood behind what the government had done so far. There hadn't been many other countries that had managed to kill so many of its citizens through negligence and indifference, so that was something of which we should all be proud. Besides, why was the Labour leader standing up and asking him all these difficult questions when he could easily have been more supportive?

This left Starmer rather perplexed, as he had a copy of a letter he had written to the prime minister a fortnight ago offering to help find a solution to the reopening of schools, to which he had not yet received a reply. 'Um . . . er,' said the floundering Boris. He had rung him back. Except he hadn't. He had merely spoken to all the opposition leaders in a joint conference call.

There was something almost pathetic about Boris pleading for people to trust him at the very moment he was lying. Starmer merely pointed out that trust had to be earned, and returned to the charge sheet. Why had Johnson eased lockdown restrictions when the woman in charge of track and trace, on which the new guidance was predicated, had said the programme wouldn't be fully functional till the end of the month? Why had the guidelines been altered when the threat was still stuck at level 4?

By now it was clear that Starmer had got under Boris's skin, and Johnson began to visibly fall apart as he tugged at his hair, tried to prevent his chin from wobbling and angrily jabbed his finger. A prime minister unable to differentiate between being picked on and being subjected to the bare minimum of democratic scrutiny. For Boris, even the most modest of criticism is interpreted as a personal betrayal. He might not be very good, but he was doing his very best, and it was about time the Labour leader and the rest of the country expressed their gratitude for that.

As so often, the leaders' exchanges ended with Boris doing a U-turn on government policy. If you had to guess from PMQs who was running the country, then you'd have to say it was Starmer. Only the previous day, Johnson had insisted on a three-line whip in support of Jacob Rees-Mogg's plans to institutionalise discrimination into the workings of the Commons. Now it sounded very much as if he had had a change of mind. Which had meant that much of Tuesday's proceedings had been as big a waste of time as MPs queueing up for 90 minutes to deprive absent MPs of a vote.

Not that queueing was necessarily a bad thing, Boris ad-libbed. The public had queued for Ikea, so it was right for MPs to get their knees dirty and queue to vote as well. Even though there was a fully functional alternative up and running already. It's getting harder and harder to know where satire ends and reality starts.

Boris breathed a sigh of relief when Starmer's six questions came to an end, but there was no let-up. The SNP's Ian Blackford twice asked Boris to condemn President Trump's handling of the riots in the US – teargassing peaceful protesters to get a photo op in front of a church had been a particular low point – and twice the prime minister declined. Even Theresa May got in on the act by asking a Brexit question he couldn't answer. How the Tory benches could do with her at PMQs right now.

The truth is that Boris is a beaten man even before he stands up to speak at the dispatch box. He knows that. Keir knows that. Worst of all, the country knows that. The shouting is all just empty white noise. A distraction from his own limitations. And at a time of national crisis, you can't get away with putting that on the side of a bus.

Fall guy Shapps takes turn to promote UK as 'world-beater' in stupidity

4 JUNE 2020

A few days ago, the prime minister announced that he was doing away with the daily coronavirus briefings at weekends. It was just getting too hard to find cabinet ministers who were prepared to give up their Saturdays and Sundays – even the ever-loyal 'cut out and keep' Tory boy pastiche, Robert Jenrick, was playing hard to get – and Boris Johnson sure as hell couldn't be bothered to do it himself.

It can't be long before No. 10 pursues its dream of reducing the number still further, if Thursday's showing is anything to go by. One – two at a push – a week would be just about ideal. A win–win situation that would cut the workload and save the daily embarrassment of a minister having to explain that the government really didn't have much of a clue what it was doing and was just making up policy on the hoof.

This is no reflection on Grant Shapps, the delegated fall guy for Thursday's press briefing. Shapps may not be the brightest kid on the block, but he's always been one of the more enthusiastic, and by cabinet standards has so far had a reasonable coronavirus war. He's by and large managed to curb his natural tendency to smile when reading out the death statistics, and he's put in more than his fair share of shifts in trying to make news out of something that is either a non-event or a government PR disaster.

But even the transport secretary is now running on fumes. The sheer pointlessness of his existence is now getting to him. And understandably so. Though he tries to maintain the jaunty, upbeat exterior of a man who just can't wait to upgrade the A66, his shoulders are now permanently slumped and he looks dead behind the eyes. Too much more of this and he's going to crack and do a runner. Luckily, he's got plenty of aliases lined up for his new life. Bye-bye, Grant. Hello, Michael Green.

Having rattled through a few slides – astonishingly, the one that showed that on the previous day the UK death total had been higher than the rest of the EU27 combined had gone missing – Shapps moved on to his 'breaking news' announcement. It had just come to his attention that there was a nasty disease called coronavirus going round, so from 15 June – might as well let a few more people die rather than doing it immediately – everyone on public transport was going to have to wear face coverings.

Well, hello. Not only had many people, including London's mayor, Sadiq Khan, been calling for such measures for weeks now, most other countries had made it law a month ago. But Grant was adamant. The UK had a reputation to maintain as the country that took measures long after they had become blindingly obvious to everyone else. It was this kind of inaction that made the UK a 'world-beater' in international stupidity.

Still, Shapps could see some light at the end of the tunnel. One way out of these daily press briefings would be simply to broadcast those of other European countries that had taken place weeks ago. Just imagine the possibilities. Rather than wasting his time today, we could have replayed the press conference of a month ago in which the Spanish transport secretary announced the compulsory wearing of face masks on public transport – only dubbed into English with Grant's voice. Put like this, no minister would ever need to appear in public again.

There was a caveat, though. Face coverings alone wouldn't be enough to stop the coronavirus, so it was still necessary for people not to make unnecessary journeys and to work from home wherever possible. This from a man who had literally queued for 90 minutes on Tuesday afternoon to take part in a vote to deny fellow MPs from having a vote or taking part in parliamentary proceedings because they had health issues, caring responsibilities, large distances to travel or were self-isolating. And all this just to indulge Jacob Rees-Mogg's ongoing public-school fantasies of entitled omnipotence.

Even when challenged on this by journalists, Shapps didn't seem to think there was anything wrong in the government implementing a three-line whip to break its own public health guidelines and put MPs and parlia-mentary staff at risk. 'Er,' said Shapps. 'We were getting behind with secondary legislation.' Then learn to use a Zoom meeting like almost everyone in the country. There's nothing to stop a committee of MPs from scru-tinising legislation online. But what Jakey wants, Jakey must have. After all, whose fault is it if you don't have a second London home and a fleet of nannies?

Grant had no answer to any of the other questions. He didn't know what advice the government may have for BAME people. He didn't know why we had still been sending hospital patients into care homes without being tested in the middle of April.

There was just time for the transport secretary to

make it clear that no one was going anywhere anytime soon. Either at home or abroad. For a start, people were forbidden from staying overnight in another home, so UK holidays were out of the question. And there was no point in people getting worked up about Priti Patel having introduced a quarantine on air travel at least six weeks too late, at a time when it would be largely ineffective, because government advice was that no one should go anywhere by air anyway. So all summer holidays were cancelled, and no harm had been done. That was the brilliance of having someone really stupid as home secretary.

Shapps quickly curtailed any other questions. The Italian transport secretary was due on TV in a few minutes, and it would be handy for Grant to know what he would be announcing in a month or so's time.

* * *

It wasn't just the coronavirus with which the government was struggling. After the murder of George Floyd by a policeman in Minneapolis, Black Lives Matter protests had kicked off all over the world. In the UK, protesters had pulled down a statue of Edward Colston, a Bristolian former slave trader, and the government found itself on the back foot in the culture wars. As it soon would be over footballer Marcus Rashford's campaign to extend free school meals, too. This became a summer of U-turns, though the government's response was to insist that everything was going entirely to plan. Matt Hancock insisted a death rate of 60,000 – when the chief medical officers had said 20,000 would be a 'good result' – and a YouGov poll showing the UK joint bottom with Mexico in an international survey of approval ratings for its handling of the pandemic were things of which to be proud. The UK had done the right thing at the right time, he insisted. The rest of Europe must have been mightily relieved they had chosen to do the wrong thing at the wrong time instead and somehow avoided the UK's disastrous public health outcomes.

Williamson can hardly fiddle the science when he can't count to two

9 JUNE 2020

There are limits to how you can fiddle the science. Only yesterday Matt Hancock had come up with the brilliant idea that the reproduction rate – the R rate – didn't much matter anyway, after it had stubbornly refused to drop from between 0.7 and 0.9. Today, though, Gavin Williamson had to bow to the inevitable. No matter how he looked at it, two metres was never going to be less than two metres. Not even if, as Jacob Rees-Mogg had suggested, you tried turning it into feet and inches.

The education secretary had even pleaded with his scientific advisers, begging them to say that two metres were actually only one metre. Or, at a push, 1.5 metres. But after months of finding their work being corrupted by the government to suit its own ends, the scientists dug their heels in. The social-distancing requirement would still be set at two metres.

On a few occasions in the past, Williamson has given flashes of the panache that won him fireplace salesman of the year in two consecutive years in 2006 and 2007, but today he was very much the bullied chemistry supply teacher as he had to explain to the Commons that he had badly miscalculated how quickly some children would be returning to school. His promise that all primary-school children would get at least some time in school before the summer holidays had been an error.

When Gavin had done the maths, he had been certain he could get at least 30 children into a classroom, but that was before he learned that it wasn't practical to suspend at least half the class from the ceiling in order for all the children to maintain a safe social distance from each other. So now he was having to work on the basis of just 15 children at most in any one classroom at any given time, which meant that at least half the rest of the kids would have to stay at home. Which rather put the kibosh on the rest of the summer term for all those year groups not in the first wave of returnees. Not that all those who had been due to restart school the previous week had done so, but that was another story . . .

Let's deconstruct the extent of Gavin's idiocy a little

further. Donald Rumsfeld struggled with both the known unknowns and the unknown unknowns. The education secretary failed to even get to grips with the known knowns. Williamson knew back in March that there was a coronavirus pandemic that had caused all schools to close. He knew that meant that all children would have to be home-schooled after a fashion and that the vulnerable and less well-off would be likely to fall behind their peers. Gavin also knew that at some point the lockdown measures would be eased gradually. The only thing he didn't know was that two metres could not be rounded down to three feet. Which is the one thing that almost every primary-school-aged kid did know.

So how did the education secretary use the two and a half months to prepare for schools reopening? By doing next to nothing. All Gav had to say for himself was that he would be following the science, he hoped more kids would get back to school once teachers had had more time to prepare, and that with any luck all schools would be fully open again by September. Though nobody should bank on it.

The shadow education secretary, Rebecca Long-Bailey, was almost lost for words in reply. Where to start? An apology to the teaching unions, whom the government had blamed last week for so many schools failing to open on time for the three year groups due back. Headteachers had been screaming about the difficulties of social distancing for weeks, but no one had listened. Even parents had been more clued up than the Department for Education and had refused to allow their kids back until they were sure it was safe.

But we were where we were, so Long-Bailey did try to offer some useful tips on what to do next. More local-ised support for children whose schools might be locked down again if the R rate went above 1 in their areas. A full programme of summer schools, free access to the internet, free school meals over the summer holidays. Anything to reduce the inevitable growth in inequal-ity that six months and more missed formal education would bring about.

A few sycophantic stooges, such as Tory Danny Kruger, apart, MPs from all sides piled in. Just how had the education secretary let things get this bad? This wasn't just bad management, it was a national humilia-tion that would affect kids for years to come. Gav looked more crestfallen than apologetic. The natural response of someone who still wasn't quite aware of just how awful things really were.

There would be some kind of summer schooling, but he probably wouldn't be able to say what exactly until the autumn. He wouldn't be offering free school meals because it would be good for kids to either lose weight or learn useful shoplifting skills. And exams would defi-nitely be taking place next summer, regardless of how much schooling anyone had got. The GCSE maths syl-labus would include a question on what percentage of children could be expected to know stuff they hadn't been taught.

But all was not lost, Gavin said desperately. He had already handed out 100,000 free laptops and was planning to dole out another 230,000 in the coming months, by which time it would hopefully be too late for some kids to catch up on the lessons they had missed. 'That's great,' said Lib Dem Layla Moran. But the chair of the education select committee had already pointed out that there were 700,000 children with no access to laptops. So by her reckoning that still left 370,000 kids education-free.

Ga opened and closed his mouth, before saying nothing. Moran just shook her head. She was wasting her breath. Given that the education secretary can barely count to two, it was expecting far too much of him to cope with subtracting large numbers.

Johnson's global Britain fantasies offer little distraction from school meals own goal

16 JUNE 2020

Things fall apart. So what would you do? The Office for National Statistics has just announced a rise in unemployment of 600,000, with many more expected to be out of work in the coming months. The economy has tanked by 20%. The UK has turned into a world leader in corona-virus deaths per head of population. The Manchester United forward Marcus Rashford has just skipped past the defence of Grant Shapps and Thérèse Coffey to set up the prime minister with a tap-in own goal on free school meals. You're also worried that Harry Kane will now enter the Brexit talks and nutmeg you with an extension to the transition period.

Ordinarily, you would expect Boris Johnson to do nothing. Partly because he's naturally lazy and the idea of leaving Downing Street to sort out the chaos brings him out in a cold sweat. But partly because Boris is at his best when he says nothing at all. He's yet to find a situation that he can't make worse by opening his mouth.

On this occasion, the prime minister chose to deal with the ongoing shitshow by going to the Commons to make an entirely unnecessary statement on his proposals to merge the Department for International Development with the Foreign Office. Just imagine: you're in the middle of the worst global health pandemic for 100 years, the economy is falling apart all around you, children are going hungry, and the most important item on your agenda is an entirely pointless departmental merger that no one except a few Tory ultras was calling for.

Boris did his best to talk up the futile exercise by calling it Global Britain, but the longer he spoke, the more it became clear the Britain he had in mind was Little Britain. Only without the jokes, but keeping the casual racism. It was something of a surprise he didn't reprise his 'picaninnies with watermelon smiles'.

He was fed up with the poorest countries treating us like 'a giant cashpoint in the sky', or taking the money and then chopping people's heads off. That kind of largesse was very late-1990s. Now was the time for the lazy scroungers to give us something back in return. If they wanted the dosh, then they had better start doing as they are told.

Opposition MPs were predictably outraged, denouncing the merger as both a diversionary tactic and a chance not just to cut the foreign aid budget, but also to redirect it to richer countries of more strategic influence. Tory MPs were rather more indulgent. For some this was a welcome end to a department they had never seen the point of, while others sought reassurances that this wasn't just an opportunity to be less generous to the poorest countries.

'Absolutely not,' Boris replied. Just trust me. The rearrangement of the deckchairs was purely an administrative convenience. The faces of Anne-Marie Trevelyan and Dominic Raab, seated further along the front bench, rather gave the lie to this. The DfID secretary looked inconsolable, while the foreign secretary appeared ecstatic at his land grab.

But trust him the Tory MPs did. Though why was another matter, given that his word is now officially meaningless. Only the day before he'd insisted there would be no U-turn on free school meals, and he'd happily allowed cabinet ministers to die on that hill defending it in public.

Not that he gave a toss about people like Shapps or Coffey. They were merely expendable extras orbiting Planet Boris. They had it coming. It wasn't just ambition that made anyone accept a cabinet job; it was also their total absence of self-worth. Boris had spent his whole life lying to his family, his friends and latterly the country, so why should he suddenly start telling the truth now? If he had a therapist, he'd probably lie to her too. Not just for the hell of it, but because he might genuinely fall apart if he told the truth. The shame would be just too much.

Sensing that he might be fighting something of a losing battle on the distractions – when even David Cameron thinks you've screwed up, then you really are having a bad day – Boris popped up again at the Downing Street press conference as a further diversionary tactic. He hasn't yet learned the value of quitting when you're no further behind. But if he was hoping that by standing next to the scientist who had completed the first success-ful trial (one part funded by DfID, the very department he had just axed – some things you just can't make up) of a steroid that reduced coronavirus mortality rates for those in hospital some of the glory would rub off on him, then he was in for a disappointment.

The first few questions were all on his embarrassment at being shamed into the free school meals U-turn by a 22-year-old footballer who'd shown more integrity over the course of a couple of days than Boris had managed in a lifetime. Johnson's pretence that he had only heard about Rashford sometime that morning fooled no one.

As for the departmental merger, Boris was adamant that he was doing it at a time when he could maximise Britain's influence abroad. As in at the very time when the prime minister was giving an object lesson in how not to govern a country. But maybe it was all just a cunning plan. Rather than handing out cash to countries, such as Tanzania, soon they would be feeling sorry for us and giving us overseas aid instead. It was the dialectics of international development. To Make Britain Great Again you first had to ensure the country was a global laughing stock.

UK ministers show how 'world-beating' they are all over again

18 JUNE 2020

For months now the government has been prefacing all its coronavirus briefings as world-beating, when the only thing in which we appeared to be global leaders was our mortality rates. But now I'm beginning to think Boris Johnson and his cabinet may have been on to something after all. Because it's beginning to look more and more as if we are genuine world-beaters, if only in total incompetence.

Check out the evidence. In Johnson we have a prime minister who lumbers from one screw-up to the next, blinded to his own failures by a narcissism that borders on the sociopathic. On Thursday, he was meeting President Macron to celebrate the 80th anniversary of De Gaulle's speech to the French Resistance. Let's hope he didn't give Macron a copy of his book on why Churchill was exactly like Boris, in which he basically wrote off De Gaulle as completely useless.

Then we have Dominic Raab, a foreign secretary who knows so little about foreign affairs and Black Lives Matter that he thought taking the knee was something out of *Game of Thrones*. At this rate it would come as no surprise to find that Gavin Williamson had been labouring under the impression that the free school meals campaign had been inspired by *Grange Hill*. What did we do to deserve politicians quite so dim as this?

But all the recent U-turns and moronic posturing are as nothing compared to the ongoing humiliation of Matt Hancock. Poor Matt. He started out with so many good intentions of being a better health secretary than his two predecessors, Andrew Lansley and Jeremy Hunt, but now just finds himself a worthy addition to the confederacy of dunces. His ambition easily outstrips his natural abilities and he merely lurches from crisis to crisis. You can see it in his eyes. His enthusiasm has been replaced by deep suspicion of everyone around him. He also looks dead on his feet. Mattbeth doth murder sleep.

It was sod's law, of course, that Matt was sent out to take the Downing Street press conference on the day that both the latest fairly rubbish human test-and-trace figures were published and the 'world-beating' app that had been promised for 1 June was finally consigned to the dustbin. Yet Hancock accepted his role and grudgingly took centre stage with Dido Harding, the chief executive of Test and Trace. There is no indignity that Boris could inflict that Matt wouldn't willingly suck up just to be allowed to keep his job for a few days or weeks longer, because he doesn't have the self-worth to face Johnson down.

Matt took a few deep breaths and tried to start off on an optimistic note. Although there was as yet no vaccine for the coronavirus, he had bought up massive supplies of all the ones that were being trialled, just on the off-chance that one of them happened to work. It was as good as an open invitation for any snake-oil salesman to come hammering on the Department of Health's door. Then Matt moved on to the figures for the human test and trace, which even he couldn't spin in a positive light as it appeared that the system was missing well over half of the people with the coronavirus.

Then he steadied himself and tackled the unhappy app situation head-on. He had discovered months ago that the 'world-beating' UK app was actually useless as it couldn't connect with Apple phones, so he had secretly set up a second programme with Apple and Google to see if they could make their systems more effective. The Germans and Koreans might be happy with the distance at which the Apple system operated, but he wasn't.

Here we came to the real genius of Hancock's cunning plan. Because faced with the choice of testing a system on the Isle of Wight that everyone knew didn't work or one that could possibly be improved, Matt had opted to waste several months testing the one that was a complete non-starter.

Brilliant. This was 'world-beating' science at its absolute best. Testing the useless one was spearheading the international effort to show other countries precisely what not to do. It was an act of supreme 'world-beating' self-sacrifice for the UK to take one for the global team. The 60,000 Brits who have died of Covid-19 could rest assured they hadn't done so in vain.

Inevitably, Matt found himself struggling with the questions from journalists. All he could do was try to pretend that the 'world-beating' app had never been that important – 'the cherry on Dido's cake' – and that people shouldn't be too worried if it wasn't working properly until sometime in the late autumn at the earliest. This after both Boris and Matt had been insistent that the app was key to relaxing lockdown restrictions, which was already taking place. It was beginning to sound as if the prime minister and health secretary were actively trying to kill people. Mattbeth doth murder more than sleep.

In desperation, Matt handed over to Harding. Unfortunately, Dido is an equally unreliable narrator, having not had tremendous success with data breaches at TalkTalk and giving the go-ahead for the Cheltenham Festival a week after many scientists had been pleading for a lockdown. The baroness is one of that elite club of chief executives who consistently manage to fail upwards. So her insistence that though the test-and-trace figures were basically crap they were still better than nothing wasn't as reassuring as it might have been.

The briefing ended in an uneasy truce, with Matt struggling to contain his tetchiness. There's only so much embarrassment even he can take. What he needed was a 'world-beating' hero on his side. If only he had a number for Daniel Rashford.

* * *

As the summer progressed, the UK started to ease its lockdown rules. 'In line with the science,' the government insisted, though many thought 'in line with the economy' was just as convincing an explanation. All non-essential retailers opened on 15 June, two-metre social-distancing rules had become one-metre-plus on 23 June, and everyone was gearing up for a full reopening – including pubs – on 4 July.

Trust me, I'm Mr Fun: Boris Johnson loosens England's lockdown

23 JUNE 2020

This was Boris Johnson's ideal day out in the Commons. For someone whose whole life seems to have been spent trying to explain his way out of awkward situations, the prime minister is notably averse to confrontation and passing on bad news. He is the country's Mr Fun. The Cheerer-Upper-in-Chief. The Mr Motivator who lets the good times roll.

So a statement on relaxing many of the country's lockdown rules was just up his street. After more than three months of more or less solitary confinement, England – Scotland, Northern Ireland and Wales are following a more cautious approach – was more or less open for business again. Households could meet, shagging could resume. The Boris bonus. Pubs and restaurants would be back in business, after a fashion – Boris was a little hazy on the details – as would hairdressers and some campsites and outdoor attractions. Boom times for model villages.

'The long national hibernation is over,' he declared, looking rather more priapic – no greater love hath any man than Boris for himself – than he has in recent weeks. And even though he was at pains to urge caution in following his approach, as the virus was an opportunistic bugger – it takes one to know one – he was still unable to contain his optimism and general bonhomie. This was a day of national celebration, not one for the gloomsters and doomsters.

In reply, Keir Starmer broadly welcomed the easing of the restrictions, though he did say it would be handy to see all the scientific evidence on which it was based and for the track-and-trace system to be working rather more effectively. Starmer also confirmed that it was safe for some children to go back to school now – something he could have said last week and saved himself some grief – which allowed Boris to break off from acting like the Special One and score a few petty party political points. The prime minister also claimed there was no country in the world that had an effective track-and-trace app, something with which several countries would disagree. But then a liar is going to lie.

This was rather the point of the rest of the debate. Trust me, said Boris. I know I have lied about a lot of things in the past, but I am telling the truth this time. And a surprisingly large number of MPs were prepared to take him at his word. Their constituents were getting fed up with lockdown, businesses were going under, and with the infection rate apparently falling it was time to give people and the economy a break. 'Always Look on the Bright Side of Life' is a catchy number.

Not everyone went home happy, though. Liberal Democrat Ed Davey wondered if, since we were firmly on the road to recovery, now would be a good time to have a national inquiry into what had gone wrong and why the UK had had one of the highest mortality rates in the world. Boris shook his head.

Tory Greg Clark wanted to know if cricket could also return. 'No,' said Boris, firmly. Because it was played with a ball. Unlike football, which started up a week ago. Even when he's trying to be serious, Boris can't help but sound like someone who is making up policy on the hoof.

As if to underline the fact that relentless cheerfulness was to be the order of the day, within minutes of ending his statement Boris declared that from tomorrow there would be no more daily Downing Street press conferences. The virus was now under control and Britain was getting back to normal, so why should he or other members of the cabinet be subjected to tricky questions from the public and the media?

The season's Downing Street finale ended as the first episode had opened, with Boris flanked by Chris Whitty and Patrick Vallance. The prime minister was rather more subdued without a live audience, but his message was essentially the same. Thanks to the resolve of the British public, not to mention the Herculean efforts of the government, only 60,000 people had died, and it was now time for the survivors to start concentrating on living again.

The chief medical officer and chief scientific adviser were noticeably much more guarded. They have both long since tired of being used as human shields for the government's incompetence and weren't going to make that mistake again. All they had done was spell out the risks; it had been the politicians who had taken the decisions.

It had been their assessment that if everyone acted entirely as they should and took proper precautions, then the risk of being one metre apart would be much the same as at two metres. But the chances of everyone behaving responsibly – especially when pissed – were just about zero, and so we would definitely be in for an increase in infections.

The longer the briefing went on, the more socially distanced Whitty and Vallance became from the prime minister. Had it gone on much longer, there would have been a fair chance they would have reversed their tacit endorsement of the end of lockdown and shouted, 'Don't trust him. He's not worth it.'

The BBC's Laura Kuenssberg asked if the prime minister would accept responsibility if everything went tits up and rates of infections and deaths increased significantly. Of course he would, Boris insisted. There's a first time for everything, I suppose.

Boris, the narcissists' narcissist, flails wildly as PMQs exposes cracks

24 JUNE 2020

What a difference a day makes. On Tuesday, Boris Johnson had been in his comfort zone. The Mr Bright Side telling the Commons more or less what it wanted to hear and getting little pushback, even from opposition MPs. The saviour releasing the country from months of hibernation. Trusting everyone to still observe the essentials of social distancing, even while they were getting pissed in newly opened pubs and bars.

Prime minister's questions, though, exposes Boris's fallibilities. Not because he is too lazy to properly prepare and isn't nearly as clever as he imagines himself to be – though both of those things are true – but because the very idea causes his psyche to go into meltdown. Johnson is the narcissists' narcissist. He believes in his inalienable right to do whatever he pleases. Even the merest hint of a challenge is an insult to his fragile ego.

Someone more self-aware might realise that the coronavirus is nowhere near half done. That mistakes have been made and others may well be in the future. That the pandemic can make a fool of anyone, and a degree of humility might be in order if he is to keep the country onside in the weeks and months ahead. People can forgive a lot if they feel they aren't being taken for mugs. But for Boris any admission of failure or liability is a psychological impossibility.

Asking Boris to take responsibility for his own actions is pointless. He just can't do it, because he is the centre of his own universe, locked into his own closed system of thought. What he wants, he must have. So it follows that whatever he does must automatically be right. People who disagree with him or are no longer useful to him are easily discarded as inconveniences.

The trouble is that Boris can dump wives, mistresses, ministers and friends, but he just can't get rid of Keir Starmer. For the first time in his life, Johnson has come up against an immovable object. And rather than accept the inevitable, Boris has merely allowed himself to regress.

Initially, he saw the Labour leader as a mild inconvenience – an unwelcome intrusion into his alternative reality – but after discovering that he couldn't make him go away with mockery and a few cheap gags, and by trying to turn the session into an interrogation of Starmer, his feelings have turned to hatred. Keir has got under his opponent's skin. Somewhere in Boris's subconscious he knows that Starmer is both better briefed and a great deal sharper, and he can't bear it. So all he can do is lash out, flailing wildly, tilting at windmills.

Part of Starmer's skill is to keep things simple. His questions have a logic that even a 10-year-old can follow. It's just a shame that Boris is still stuck in the toddler age of development. The Labour leader began by pointing out that easing restrictions was all very well, providing that the track-and-trace system was functioning properly. Which at present it wasn't, as it was missing two-thirds of cases. So how did the government propose to get it working properly by 4 July? Boris was outraged. How could the person who had offered him cautious support the day before now dare to challenge him on the detail? That was the kind of disloyalty only he was allowed.

The Labour leader just kept plugging away. This wasn't obstruction, it was constructive criticism, he observed, as he reiterated the point that he was quoting from the government's own data and wasn't interested in the one-third of the system that was working. He then moved on to the app, which had been downgraded in the past few weeks from 'critical' and 'world-beating' to 'additional support', before observing that the prime minister had misled the house on the child poverty figures last week, and would he mind correcting himself? Just for the record.

All that Boris had to offer was histrionics and lies. Gestures of feigned 'What me, guv?' innocence, combined with blatant untruths. Boris still labours under the impression that if you tell a lie often enough, then it somehow becomes true. But what might work on the campaign trail on the sides of buses just doesn't cut it when you're supposed to be the prime minister during the greatest health crisis for a century.

We reached full-on meltdown shortly after Johnson claimed he had never said the app would be anything other than 'icing on the cake' – since Boris begins each day as a *tabula rasa*, he must think the rest of us are equally amnesiac – when he went back to the tactic of asking Starmer about schools, which had been moderately successful the week before. Only this time it failed dismally as Starmer had long since answered it.

The few dozen Tory backbenchers in the chamber kept their heads down. They were as embarrassed as Boris would have been had he the capacity for that level of empathy. It's slowly dawning on most Tories that Boris just isn't up to the job, as they witness their leader unravel at PMQs week after week. Nor do many have much faith in his ability to make the right calls at the right time with the pandemic. And having used up what little goodwill he might have had – Boris has never bothered to conceal his contempt for most, make that all, of his colleagues – his support is dwindling.

Too many more PMQs like this and something will start to give. And as Boris is incapable of change, then it can't be long before his suitability for the job comes under scrutiny from his own party. It was probably always inevitable that the person who would ultimately destroy Boris was Boris himself. But Starmer is doing a great job of exposing his faults. There is a crack in everything. That's how the light gets in.

Well, that went well. The government's guidance to stay clear of the seaside went largely unheeded when the sun came out – the beaches were all rammed – and Leicester went into local lockdown even before the rest of the country had reopened. Meanwhile, in Westminster Keir Starmer and Boris Johnson had responded very differently to crises within their own parties. The Labour leader had unceremoniously sacked Rebecca Long-Bailey at the first whiff of her having endorsed anti-Semitism. Boris, though, had refused to sack his housing minister, Robert Jenrick, who, after meeting one-time pornographer Richard Desmond at a Tory fundraising dinner and exchanged phone numbers, had illegally intervened to push through Dirty Des's housing development in the nick of time to save him from a £50 million tax liability. If Jenrick had an ounce of decency, he would have resigned; if Boris had a hint of decency, he would have sacked him.

Boz the Bluster gets hammered in PMQs 'whack-a-mole'

1 JULY 2020

Boz the Bluster. Can he fix it? On the evidence of his latest outing at prime minister's questions, the answer is a categorical 'no'. Right now, you wouldn't trust Boris Johnson to get himself dressed in the morning, let alone get dragged around the park by Dilyn the dog.

Six months into his term of office, he already looks a spent force. A man desperately playing catch-up as he tries to respond to events that are out of his control.

'We are the builders, you are the blockers,' he said towards the end of his reply – if you can call it that – to Keir Starmer's final question. 'We are the doers, you are the ditherers.'

Even the most loyal Tory backbenchers in the chamber looked taken aback by that. Labour had not had anything to block – even assuming they wanted to – as the Tories had not built anything in the past decade. And when it comes to dithering, the prime minister has elevated it into an art form.

Dithering is what Boris does best. He is a man who wants to be liked, someone who tries to keep his failings and infidelities hidden to avoid any unpleasantness or confrontation. So the decisions he does make are invariably made too late. Take coronavirus: while other countries were going into lockdown, Boris just let things roll for another 10 days, waiting on a miracle that never came. Partly because he didn't want to be responsible for the upheaval that would follow, but also because he didn't want Carrie to have to cancel her baby shower at Chequers.

Since easing lockdown restrictions, Johnson has opted for a 'whack-a-mole' strategy of targeting localised outbreaks. It's also the new tactic he has adopted for PMQs. Only in this instance it is him that's the mole. Boris would never admit it in person – far too proud and narcissistic – but part of his subconscious appears to have accepted that he has met his match in the Labour leader.

In his previous outings against Starmer he has run through all the familiar defensive tropes from his Oxford Union debating repertoire – scorn, sarcasm, bluster, answering a different question – but has on every occasion been comprehensively outplayed. So all that's left for him is to try and play dumb by sticking his head out of the hole and hope he can scamper back for cover before he gets whacked.

Unfortunately, Boris is not the most nimble on his feet, and he's as bad at 'whack-a-mole' PMQs as he was at all the others. Six times he put his head above the parapet and six times he got clobbered. It was going to take more than a couple of paracetamols to deal with the headache. He was facing an entire afternoon on a morphine drip.

Starmer opened with the Leicester lockdown. How come it had taken so long to introduce the new restrictions, when there had been evidence of a local spike 11 days ago? Boris went into full blame mode. He had actually noticed the rise in infections back on 8 June and had sent more testing units to the city, but unfortunately the people of Leicester had failed to act as they should have done. The government was socially distancing itself from its people.

That wasn't quite true, the Labour leader observed.

What had actually happened was that the government hadn't shared the pillar 2 tests – the drive-through and self-testing – with the local health authority, so no one in Leicester had a clue just how bad things were.

In fact, the mayor of Leicester had confirmed exactly that on Wednesday morning. Boris had no answer other than to burble and bumble. A telltale sign that he was lying.

Thereafter it just got worse and worse for him. Starmer invited him to indulge in self-reflection – never Johnson's strongest suit – and say sorry for having been so flippant the previous week in urging the MPs of seaside towns to 'show some guts' – a comment that had provoked a major incident in Bournemouth, with an influx of 500,000 people to the beach.

'Pifflepaffle, people have to act responsibly,' he said. Right. Just as Dominic Cummings had acted responsibly on his Durham safari.

The rest was just white noise. Boz the Bluster couldn't understand why Labour wasn't giving him more applause for the 25% of people the government was managing to reach through its 'world-beating' track-and-trace system rather than negatively focusing on the 75% of people it was missing. It's hard to know which is the icing on the cake right now: the mothballed app or the track-and-trace system. All that's clear is there's not much in the way of cake to put any icing on.

So it went on as Boris appeared to disintegrate, completely losing touch with any semblance of reality. The

£5 billion infrastructure project he had announced the day before had miraculously expanded overnight into a £650 billion spending programme. That's inflation for you. 'There will be plenty of wonderful things,' he said, with characteristic penetration. The future was going to be like a bumper edition of the *Generation Game*, with towns across the country fighting over who was going to win the cuddly toy.

Nor could Johnson offer much hope on jobs. Other than the hope that companies in the hospitality and services sectors should try not to make people redundant. Still, look on the bright side. If all businesses in the entertainment industry did go bust, then their employees could retrain as apprentices and 'build, build, build'.

Boris was left to mouth empty, three-word Classic Dom slogans. And Tory MPs were left to wonder why they had never previously noticed that their emperor had no clothes.

Mattbeth fails to mask government's latest U-turn on Covid face coverings

14 JULY 2020

It can't be long before Matt Hancock's lucky pink tie springs to life and crawls away in shame. The tie and Matt have been an inseparable double act for several months now, but there's only so much humiliation even a strip of polyester can take. Matt, though, appears immune to his own hubris. Rather, he wears it as a badge of honour. A sign of his indispensability to a regime that increasingly resembles that of a failed state, lurching hopelessly from one screw-up to the next. Imagine the neediness – the lack of any self-worth – in that level of ambition.

We've long passed the point where one member of the cabinet knows what another is doing. Left hand, meet right hand. On Friday, we had Boris Johnson, having previously insisted that face masks were for wimps, saying that he thought it might be a good idea for people to wear them in shops. Though he stopped short of making it compulsory. On Sunday, Michael Gove openly contradicted the prime minister and said it was down to the British public to use their old-fashioned 'common sense'. By Monday, even the justice secretary, Robert Buckland, was hopelessly confused and declared that face masks should definitely maybe possibly be worn.

All this took place against a background of months – if not years – of research into the spread of coronaviruses in other countries, which indicated masks were an effective way of reducing the risk of infection in public places. Though apparently not in the UK. So it was almost an inevitability that come Tuesday, the government would be forced into yet another embarrassing U-turn and that the person to take the hit of making a statement in the Commons would be the health secretary himself.

Hancock began on the offensive. The government had a remarkable record in its handling of the pandemic. Remarkable, as in taking almost every key decision far too late and winding up with one of the world's highest mortality rates. Infection rates were coming down, and as long as we could all conveniently forget the recent report from the Academy of Medical Sciences that predicted a possible 120,000 deaths in a second wave in the winter, then we could all have a jolly couple of months while the lockdown was being eased.

Oh, and by the way, Matt had now decided that masks in shops were a good idea after all. Though not such a good idea that they would be introduced immediately. Far better to wait another 10 days for that, as the government had top-level intelligence that the coronavirus had declared an amnesty and wouldn't be infecting anyone before 24 July. Which will come as a huge relief to shop workers, who have a mortality risk 60–75% higher than the rest of the general population. After 24 July, there would be a £100 fine for refuseniks; before then, just a possible death penalty.

Up till now, the shadow health secretary, Jon Ashworth, has tended to give Mattbeth the benefit of the doubt and tried to offer constructive criticism in his replies to ministerial statements. But this time enough was enough. How was it that the government consistently managed to make such a balls-up of all its messaging? It had been obvious from the start that face masks in shops were a good idea, so why the delay in implementing them? And while he was about it, perhaps Hancock might like to clear up the advice on work? Because the current government position was that it was a good idea to work both at home and in the office. Perhaps everyone could split the difference and do their work on public transport instead?

Matt wasn't at all happy at being talked to like this by Ashworth. He can take any amount of shaming from his cabinet colleagues, but he can't face a reality check from the opposition, and his reply was decidedly tetchy. No one would have done better than him. Which was true. No one would have been as good an option. There wasn't much more to be said about masks in shops – no point in rubbing it in – so most Labour MPs chose to enquire about the failures of the track-and-trace system. Which only made Hancock grumpier still.

The Tory MPs mostly seemed to be under instructions to not mention the masks, though Desmond Swayne thought the whole idea of shopping in a face covering to be 'a monstrous imposition'. Presumably, it's an Englishman's right to spread germs wherever he pleases. Another Conservative, James Davies, also broke ranks – 'Don't mention the war!' – by asking if masks should now be introduced in bars and restaurants. 'No,' said Matt firmly, thereby ensuring he will be back in the Commons within a matter of days to make masks in bars and restaurants compulsory.

The only plus side for Hancock was that he wasn't the only cabinet minister having a bad day, as Oliver Dowden had earlier had to perform a U-turn on the government's decision, taken in January, to allow Huawei to build the UK's 5G network. Oliver isn't the brightest – he makes Mattbeth look positively quick-witted – and he looked understandably miserable throughout. But then he was being asked to talk pure bollocks.

It was fine to allow Huawei access till 2027 as the Chinese had given a written undertaking that they definitely wouldn't be doing any spying in the next seven years. And it had absolutely been the right thing for the government to give the go-ahead in January and then to change its mind now. No contradiction whatsoever. And certainly no pressure from the US over future trade deals. It had all been yet another calculated act to make the UK look as weak and indecisive as possible. The one thing at which the government currently excels.

Like a borderline sociopath, Johnson again misjudges the mood of the chamber

15 JULY 2020

It's become a standard strategy for Boris Johnson at prime minister's questions, ever since he got mullered in their first few outings. Unable to cope with the detail of

Keir Starmer's questions, he lashes out with diversionary tactics, either accusing the Labour leader of doing something he hasn't done, answering a completely different question or playing to the non-existent gallery of Tory backbenchers.

There's just one large spanner in the works: it's not working. Because at every PMQs Boris merely reveals more of the true character he is trying to conceal: the thin-skinned, unprepared opportunist who cannot tolerate a word of scrutiny or criticism. It's like dealing with a toddler. If you're not 100% behind him, saying how marvellous he is, then you are totally against him. There are no in-betweens. In terms of emotional development, Boris is barely out of nappies.

How else can you explain Wednesday's performance at PMQs other than as a full-on narcissistic breakdown? Starmer had started by asking about the lack of sector-specific support for aviation. Boris was outraged. Labour had broadly backed the chancellor's bail-out plans for other industries last week, so why was Starmer now choosing to make a fuss about widespread redundancies and BA's plan to fire 30,000 employees and rehire them on worse terms and conditions? This was just talking Britain down.

'The Labour leader says one thing one week and another the next,' Boris yelled, hammering on the dispatch box with his index finger in a temper tantrum. This was quite some cheek as in the last few days we've had

Michael Gove telling the Commons that there will be expensive and time-consuming post-Brexit border checks – just about the only thing we will 'build, build, build' are lorry parks – after assuring the country we would still have access to the single market. Not to mention Oliver Dowden reversing the decision to allow Huawei access to build our 5G network and poor Matt Hancock having to tidy up the mess the government had got itself into over wearing masks in shops.

Starmer looked justifiably angry but did his best to control his emotions and moved on instead to the report from the Academy of Medical Sciences that had warned the UK risked another 120,000 deaths from the coronavirus over the coming winter. Wouldn't now be a good time to make sure that the government's test-and-trace system was working properly?

Now Boris just leapt into the realms of fantasy. Aka pure Donald Trump. Our test-and-trace system was the envy of the world. The best there was. The very bestest, bigliest best. In which case the world might as well prepare for its end now, as the test-and-trace figures are getting worse by the week. Where once we were reaching 80% of the contacts – of the 25% of infected people we were managing to track – we were now down to barely 70%. At the current rate of decline, the whole system will be little better than guesswork in a few months. Or less, if Mattbeth's world-beating app makes an appearance in the meantime.

'He should be building up the system, not undermining

it,' Boris said, apparently unaware that no one had done more to reduce public confidence in the government's response to the pandemic than him. Dominic Cummings excluded. Because at every opportunity, the prime minister has done too little, too late, which is one of the main reasons why the UK death figures genuinely are world-beating.

At this point, it dawned on Starmer that Boris almost certainly hadn't read the report to which he had referred – a little slow on the uptake from the Labour leader, as the prime minister never reads any report of more than two paragraphs – so he asked him outright if he had. 'Um . . . er . . .' Boris hesitated. He was aware of the report. In the same way he is aware that he has children, but is unable to say exactly how many. And in the same way I am aware of the space–time continuum, but would be unable to explain exactly what the science meant to anyone. Though if it turned out that Boris only really existed in another parallel dimension, then I'd happily settle for that.

The Labour leader ended by basically accusing the prime minister of lying about the success of his government's response and wondering what he might like to say to the families of those who had died – and of those who would die in the future – as a result of his negligence. It was a serious, solemn question. And one that was treated as a joke, as Boris responded by saying Starmer had 'more briefs than Calvin Klein'. I'm sure that gave all the bereaved a good chuckle. The prime minister's

ability to misjudge the mood of the chamber is borderline sociopathic.

It had been yet another Johnson PMQs rocky horror
show. A travesty of its true purpose and an insult to the
country. People are dying. People are losing their jobs.
People are terrified about the future. And yet to Boris
it all still feels like a big game, where the only thing at
stake is his fragile ego. He did, when pushed by the Lib
Dems' Ed Davey, commit to a national inquiry into the
government's handling of the pandemic, but not to any
time soon. Certainly not in time to save any more lives
this winter, and certainly not before he has a chance to
shift the blame onto someone else.

At times like these, we need a leader in whom to
believe. What we've got is a prime minister who urgently
needs a therapist.

Tired of being Boris Johnson's patsy, Patrick Vallance fights back

16 JULY 2020

Yesterday Boris Johnson committed himself to a public
inquiry into the government's handling of the coronavirus pandemic. He didn't say when, though he gave the
distinct impression that the ideal time would be a long
way into the future. By when he would have had time to

line up any number of patsies to take the rap for his own failures. One of whom is sure to be the government's chief scientific adviser, Patrick Vallance.

It's fair to say that Vallance has been a little slow off the mark right from the very start of the pandemic. Not so much with the science – though he's hardly excelled at that – but with PR management. For a long time, he was under the impression that his prime role was to provide the government with independent scientific advice; it's only over the course of the last few weeks that he's realised his real function is to be a human shield for Boris. And he's clearly not happy about having been suckered in this way.

So for Vallance, a two-hour appearance before the science and technology select committee was an ideal opportunity to lay the foundations of his fightback. A chance to redirect the blame to where it really lay. And in Greg Clark, the committee chair and former cabinet minister, he had someone who was only too happy to indulge him. Boris is only just beginning to realise that for all his acolytes who fawn over every Latin word, he has some powerful enemies on the Tory back benches.

Satisfied that he was a full two metres away from the nearest committee member – there were only three of them in the room, the rest were virtual – Vallance ostentatiously removed his face mask and began to let rip. Was it still true that there had been no significant occasions on which the government had ignored the Scientific

Advisory Group for Emergencies' advice? Clark asked.

The chief scientific adviser smiled benignly. His only job was to provide the government with the scientific evidence. Which idiotic decisions happened to be taken as a result of that advice was completely up to the government. To suggest there was any correlation between the advice SAGE might have given and government policy was absurd. Any overlap could only ever be a coincidence.

Clark then gently tiptoed into trickier areas. The UK hadn't had particularly good coronavirus outcomes – a euphemism for the highest mortality rate in the world – and it was hard to find any country that particularly admired the standard of our science. How did he account for that?

'The outcomes have not been good,' Vallance agreed. But that was entirely because the UK's data flow had been poor and because our test-and-trace systems were hopelessly inadequate. He and other members of SAGE had been complaining about this to Public Health England and the Department for Health and Social Care for months, but neither body had taken a blind bit of notice. Just as he had flagged up concerns about the risk of transmission in care homes and been totally ignored.

Not that Vallance wanted to lay all the blame at the government's door. He was far too polite for that. Or possibly passive-aggressive. When you've been taken for a fool for so long, it's hard not to take some pleasure from exacting revenge. Face masks? He'd been all in favour of them long before the World Health Organization had jumped on the bandwagon. It was just that Boris hadn't been that interested in what he had had to say. But then the prime minister did have a lot of other things on his mind at the time.

The killer line came when Vallance insisted SAGE had recommended an immediate total lockdown on 16 March. A bit late in the day possibly, given the rate of infection in the UK was increasing exponentially and that dozens of other countries had already introduced lockdowns, but still a good week before Boris could be bothered to getting round to doing anything about it. But then Jockey Club director Dido Harding – soon to be chief executive of Track and Trace – had wanted the Cheltenham Festival to go ahead, and it would have been a shame for Carrie Symonds to have had to cancel her baby shower at Chequers. So, all in all, it was probably worth the 20,000 extra deaths the week's delay entailed.

By now, Vallance, normally one of the dourest, most defensive of men, looked as if he was beginning to enjoy himself. The session was developing into gestalt therapy, and he was on the brink of catharsis, all that pent-up hurt and resentment finally being allowed an outlet. Yes, things still were basically a bit shit. He couldn't understand why the government's testing programme was still so rubbish, as on current evidence Matt Hancock didn't have a prayer of reaching his winter targets. And yes, he knew that Boris was due to give a speech the following day encouraging people to go back to work, but his advice was for everyone to stay put at home.

Back in No. 10, Dominic Cummings was having a hissy fit as he wondered how to rephrase the government's advice, but Vallance was on a *Schadenfreude* high. All he had ever done was present the evidence as he saw it – even if he had been a bit slow on the uptake at times – and if the government had acted irresponsibly, then it was nothing to do with him, guv. Over to you, Boris and Matt.

Hancock had been down to appear before the committee immediately after Vallance, but Matt had wisely excused himself by giving a statement to the Commons on extending the Leicester lockdown instead. Anything to buy himself a bit of time. Because after Vallance's evidence, Mattbeth is going to need to come up with some creative answers next Tuesday. The blame game is only just beginning. And it could be the only fun thing to come out of the whole coronavirus pandemic.

Shapps feels the pain in Spain on holiday from hell

25 JULY 2020

Imagine the scene: Grant Shapps and his family had flown into Spain on Saturday lunchtime, picked up the hire car and had just settled into the self-catering villa when he chose to break the bad news. As of midnight UK time, anyone returning from Spain would have to quarantine themselves for 14 days.

'Now you tell us,' his wife and three children had chorused angrily. 'We thought you were meant to be the "air corridor" transport secretary. Did you actually know this was going to happen?'

'Well, I did get a text this morning from Matt Hancock, saying he was much enjoying his hols canoeing in England and how sorry he was to screw up our time in Spain. Though he didn't give me any exact details. But in any case, if we had cancelled our hols, then it would have looked like we'd been acting on inside information.'

'So let's get this straight. You let us all come out here knowing that we would have to be cooped up at home for a fortnight on our return. Didn't you think that some of us might have stuff arranged for when we got back? Worse still, why have you knowingly flown us to a place where we're more likely to get sick?'

'You needn't worry too much about that. Most of Spain has a far lower rate of coronavirus infection than the UK. So we're probably safer out here than back home.'

'In which case why have you put blanket quarantine restrictions on the entire country? Wouldn't it have been better just to target those regions where the infection rate had gone up?'

'Oh,' said Shapps. 'I hadn't thought of that. Michael Gove just said we had to include the whole of Spain because he's got a holiday in Ibiza booked and he rather fancied an extra two weeks lounging around at home when he gets back.'

The rest of the evening had passed in an uneasy silence. His wife was giving him the cold shoulder and the kids were on their phones, texting their friends about what a moron they had for a dad.

Things were still tense the following morning, but eventually everyone agreed to go down to the beach for lunch. On reflection, a mistake, because it was just his luck that there was one Brit who happened to recognise him, and within minutes he was being harangued by dozens of holiday-makers who were pissed off to find out their summer had been completely ruined.

Shapps's first instinct had been to try and lie his way out of it. 'I'm not Grant Shapps,' he had insisted. 'I'm Michael Green. I mean, *me llamo* Miguel Verde.' But after 20 minutes or so, he had been ground down and forced to give an informal briefing to a bunch of angry strangers. No, he couldn't give them any advice on claiming statutory sick pay or universal credit for the quarantine period. And no, he had no idea how long the self-isolation restrictions would remain in place. In fact, he was just as clueless as they were about the current situation. It had all been a bit last-minute, and the government was still making up policy on the hoof.

After a miserable lunch, Shapps and his family returned to the villa. 'There's only one way this holiday is going to work,' said his wife. 'And that's if you remain inside the compound where no one can see you for the next two weeks, while me and the kids go off in the car and try to enjoy ourselves as best we can without you.' Grant nodded meekly.

So, on Monday morning, Shapps found himself at a bit of a loose end. Out of boredom as much as curiosity, he phoned his government department.

'Look on the bright side,' said his special adviser. 'You're not the only minister who has been caught out. Paul Scully is stuck in Lanzarote.'

'Who is Paul Scully?'

'No idea. But I've been told he's been tweeting photos of a couple of beers on the Playa Dorada, along with some bollocks about people behaving confidently and sensibly.'

'So can you give me any more information about what's going on? Can't we at least open up the Canaries and the Balearics?'

''Fraid not. The Foreign Office has got it in for them too. God knows why. Nobody in Whitehall has a clue what's going on. Things are so bad they even sent Helen Whately out to do the morning media round. Besides, nobody ever listens to a word we say.'

'Well, can we try and find out where Dominic Raab is going for his holidays and impose quarantine restrictions there? Even if it's in England and it means closing down the whole of the West Country.'

Having wasted two minutes watching the video of Boris Johnson talking up the benefits of exercise, Shapps dozed off. Only to be woken a few hours later by the return of his family.

'It's no good. I've decided I'm going home on Wednesday,' he told them. 'I'm bored out of my mind on my own here.'

'Are you serious?' his wife replied. 'You mean you dragged us all out here knowing we were going to be in quarantine, and now you're going back early because of the quarantine? You can't make this stuff up. No wonder most people think everyone in government is a complete twat.'

'I'm sorry. But I think it's for the best,' Grant mumbled sheepishly. 'And I guess I might get some time off quarantine with a visit to Barnard Castle. In any case, I won't have to do any food shopping as I can take advantage of the government's obesity strategy, which will give me £10 off every Burger King Deliveroo meal.'

Just another quiet day in the home office of dedicated contact tracers

5 AUGUST 2020

29 May: An email arrives. 'Dear Sir, I am delighted to offer you a job as one of the UK's "world-beating" test-and-tracers. It will be tough, skilled work, involving dozens of phone calls each day, and your training will

begin tomorrow. Thank you again for your dedication. Together we can beat the coronavirus and bring the country back to normal by Christmas. Yours, Boris Johnson and Baroness Dido Harding.'

7th June: Another email arrives. 'Congratulations on completing your training.' I reply that I have yet to receive any training. Hear nothing back.

9th June: I email the head of training at Serco to remind her of my existence and to say that I am still awaiting instructions. This time she replies promptly to say that the training was targeted to help workers get used to long periods of doing nothing and that I need to be focused a great deal more on being patient. The less we do, the more effective we are being.

23rd June: I have yet to make a single test-and-trace call, despite having sat at home with my phone at the ready and the TV switched off for the past 14 days. I ring my local Serco HQ to check that they actually have the right number for me. They do, and confirm that I am in the weekly draw for the most productive member of staff over the course of the last week.

1st July: Sod's law. Have just invited some friends over for a barbecue when I get an alert from the test-and-trace centre to call someone. Go indoors to prepare to give the bad news that they will have to self-isolate for 14 days, only to find it is a non-existent number.

4th July: I'm now on a roll. I get a second alert and call the number, which goes straight to voicemail. I don't let this go as I don't want to be responsible for a super-spreader slipping through the net. Eventually, a man picks up and starts yelling at me. I am the twelfth person to have contacted him over the past few days, and would I please stop interrupting his quarantine?

10th July: The call centre emails to ask me what my favourite flower is. I give this a few minutes' thought and reply, 'On balance, I think I like bluebells the best. Why do you want to know?' An hour or so later, I get an out-of-office reply saying, 'To be honest, we don't give a shit one way or another what your favourite flower is. It was just a way of finding out how many of you were still monitoring your phones.'

18th July: I have seldom felt so desperate. I submit my own number to the test-and-trace database just so that someone will ring me to tell me to self-isolate. Even then no one calls. I ring the Serco human resources department. After half an hour the line goes to voicemail: 'If you are a test-and-tracer who feels their life might be entirely futile, please try calling the self-help group Test and Trace Anonymous.'

19th July: 'My name's Simon and I'm a test-and-tracer,' I say. 'Join the club,' says a woman. 'Try not to worry too much. There are thousands of us who feel the same. Some people have been doing this for months without talking to anyone. Why don't you sign up for one of our daily quizzes?' Finally, I feel like I am getting somewhere.

21st July: Totally psyched for the quiz. 'Question 1: Name the woman on the Jockey Club board who was responsible for giving this year's Cheltenham Festival the go-ahead, thereby risking the spread of the coronavirus pandemic.' Easy. Dido Harding. 'Question 2: Name the former chief executive of TalkTalk whose utter ignorance of the company was famously described as a lesson to all.' That would be Dido again. I'm beginning to think there may be a theme here.

24th July: Am given a number to ring by one of the other test-and-tracers. Big mistake. I get through to a Liam Fox, who thinks I am from the World Trade Organization. 'I'm sorry about all my hacked emails on the US–UK trade talks,' he says. 'But am I still in line to be director of the WTO?' I suggest that's unlikely. But on the upside, I tell him he doesn't have to self-isolate for 14 days. He starts blubbing, and I put the phone down gently.

26th July: I finally get to make a call that isn't a fake number, doesn't go to voicemail and hasn't been rung countless times before. As a result, I am given a €50 voucher to spend anywhere in Spain over the course of the next month.

27th July: All non-essential travel to Spain is stopped and a 14-day quarantine imposed on travellers returning from the country. Try to flog my voucher to friends stuck in Spain for €20. Get told to bugger off.

1st August: Receive a message from Boris Johnson saying all those working from home should now be working in the office. Worried, I ring the No. 10 switchboard to let them know I don't have an office. A bored receptionist says not to worry as Boris is working from his country house for the rest of the summer.

* * *

On 3 April, the Department for Education and Ofqual, England's exam regulator, had announced that pupils taking GCSEs and A-levels would have their grades awarded by a combination of teacher assessment, class ranking and past performance of their schools. By July, the education select committee was warning that there was potential bias in this system against black, Asian and minority ethnic pupils, as well as those with special needs. Even after the Scottish exam results were announced in early August, confirming just such a bias, Gavin Williamson, the secretary of state for education, insisted there would be no change in the English system.

On 7 August, the Guardian *revealed that 39% of teachers' A-level results recommendations were set to be downgraded, with those most at risk being students from comprehensive schools with significant variations in attainment over the previous three years. On 11 August, following days of protest from pupils, teachers and opposition parties, the Scottish government reinstated all downgraded exam results. Despite it being obvious to all other than Williamson that the English results were an accident waiting to happen, the secretary of state was adamant there would be no changes to the system.*

Sure enough, the English A-level results were published, with pupils from disadvantaged backgrounds being hardest hit by the standardisation process and researchers predicting that even greater discrimination would be evident in the GCSE results to be published a week later. On 15 April, Ofqual suspended its guidance on exam marking. Two days later, the government performed its own U-turn by announcing that all A-level and GCSE results would now be based solely on teacher-assessed grades. Calling this a shambles is being polite.

It's a dog's breakfast for Gavin Williamson and his owner

26 AUGUST 2020

'Do you take responsibility for what happened? Because last week my colleague on this programme, Louise Minchin, asked you several times if you had considered your resignation, and you didn't answer that then,' said *BBC Breakfast*'s Dan Walker. 'So do you take responsibility for what happened over exams and what happened in the last 24 hours over the wearing of face coverings in schools?'

'Um . . . unprecedented . . . er . . . pandemic . . .' replied Gavin Williamson, as he wittered on for 30 seconds about nothing very much.

'But do you take responsibility for the issues in your department?' Walker interrupted.

'Um . . . in terms of exam results . . . er . . . policy approach . . .' Gavin continued aimlessly.

Finally, Walker – possibly the gentlest interviewer any cabinet minister could hope to come up against – cracked. 'You're talking down the time so I don't get to ask you the questions,' he snapped. And when Walker reaches his breaking point, you know the game is up.

But then Williamson had known the game was up the night before, when he had got the phone call from the prime minister telling him he had changed his mind about face masks in schools and that he wanted him to do the Wednesday-morning media round. Even Private Pike has a humiliation threshold. It had been bad enough having to explain why he had switched to predicted A-level grades the week before; now he was going to have to come up with another reason for doing the one thing the government had said it wasn't going to do only days earlier.

'What shall I tell them this time?' Gavin had sobbed.

'How about that they've got as much chance of dying from the coronavirus as being knocked down by a car?' Boris Johnson had said.

'I'm not sure that choosing between two ways of dying is the way to go here.'

'Oh, well, I'm sure you will think of something. I'm up to my neck trying to stop that Scottish farmer from suing me for trespass. And don't worry, I'm about to appoint that right-wing Aussie lunatic Tony Abbott to the board of trade – it will be a race to the bottom to see who is the stupider, him or Liz Truss, so with any luck everyone will soon forget your latest embarrassment.'

It didn't feel that way to Private Pike as he shuffled from the *BBC Breakfast* to the *Today* studio. If he could get his arse handed to him on a plate by Walker, God knows what state he would be in by the time Mishal Husain had finished with him.

He tried to rehearse his lines mentally. It was like this. This wasn't yet another U-turn. Rather, it was a sign of clarity and consistency. The country had got used to the government constantly changing its mind on issues, so everyone would have been mentally prepared for the latest switch of policy. Had the government actually stuck to what it had said it was going to do, then everyone would have been totally confused. Besides, no one – apart from a whole load of twitchy Tory MPs, such as Huw Merriman and Charles Walker, who were demanding he made a bad decision and stuck with it – wanted a government that wasn't prepared to do something different to what it had promised.

'At every stage we listen to the latest scientific advice,' Gavin began, sounding more confident than he felt.

Now it was Husain's turn to be confused. Her

understanding was that the World Health Organization had issued guidelines stating that it was beneficial for secondary students to wear face coverings in areas of schools where social distancing could not be guaranteed. So how come the deputy chief medical officer, Jenny Harries, had said on Monday there was no strong evidence for them? Hell, even Alok Sharma, the business secretary whose signature move was never to commit himself to anything that might be construed as news, had confirmed just the day before that masks in schools were a definite no-no.

'Ah, let me be clear,' said Gavin. He hadn't said how quickly he would follow the scientific advice, and England had a strong track record of reacting later than everyone else. That was why we had a coronavirus mortality rate to be proud of. Besides, it was no big deal. It was only for schools in lockdown areas, and on no account were children going to be wearing masks in the classroom. At which point headteachers of all schools everywhere made a note to prepare for pupils wearing masks the whole time.

By now, Private Pike was prepared to commit himself to anything and promised that all schools would definitely return in September. He had no idea if this was true, but he no longer much cared as he knew he was in line for the sack within a month or two regardless. Husain cut to the chase.

'Do you actually want to stay in the job?' she said, her voice finally betraying a hint of sympathy for the hapless education secretary.

'I love the job. It's the best job in government.' The teachers at his comprehensive school had done a brilliant job in helping him to achieve what he wanted in life. Even if the rest of the country was wishing they had done a slightly worse job and that fireplace salesman of the year 2006 remained Gav's career highlight.

There was still just time for him to land Sally Collier, the outgoing Ofqual chief executive, in the brown stuff before he was done for the day. She had been a goner since the moment he expressed his full confidence in her, and surely no one would ever find out that his department had been more concerned about grade inflation than the impact of an algorithm that disadvantaged pupils from poorer areas? And even if they did, they would assume he had meant the opposite.

Gav also considered mentioning that Jonathan Slater, the most senior civil servant in the Department for Education, would also be getting the sack later in the day for the exams chaos. Heads must roll. It was time for someone to show real leadership in the department, the prime minister had told him earlier in the day. And there was no chance of that real leadership coming from Gavin or Boris. Their only real discernible function was to be at best a distraction and at worst a waste of space.

Still, at least he wasn't the only one having a tricky day, as around lunchtime Boris found himself addressing a group of students in a school library. All of whom looked unimpressed and blank throughout. Every one of the PM's gags fell flat, and his attempt to blame their exam results on 'a mutant algorithm' – one that he had previously championed – was met with outright hostility. It's not just Walker and Husain who know bullshit when they hear it.

Boris left flailing as his limitations become clear for all to see

2 SEPTEMBER 2020

Boris Johnson's complete lack of shame has long been one of his defining narcissistic traits. His willingness to betray family, friends and colleagues for short-term personal gain is common knowledge. In much the same way, his lack of competence – his inability to grasp basic details – had also been priced into the equation, as no one on the Tory benches much cared. It was just Boris being Boris.

But something has changed over the course of the summer. Johnson is no longer seen as a man with the winning touch. Quite the reverse, in fact. Many Conservatives are slowly waking up to the fact that he may be a liability. Many prime ministers have discovered that being in the top job requires a different skill- and mindset to that of getting the top job. The difference with Boris is that he shows no sign of being willing to learn how to adapt to the change. Rather, he appears to be getting worse and worse at being prime minister. Limitations that are increasingly being exposed in laziness, short-temperedness and forgetfulness.

Prime minister's questions are often dismissed as a piece of performance theatre. Something only of interest to those inside the Westminster bubble. And there is some truth in that. But they also offer a window into a leader's soul, revealing qualities such as empathy, wit, intelligence and humility.

And on all counts Boris is failing miserably. His inability to gauge not just the mood of the House of Commons but that of the nation also is borderline sociopathic. It is as if he is holed up in a bunker, surrounded by yes-men – there are almost no women in Boris's inner circle – telling him only the things he wants to hear.

By contrast, Keir Starmer is learning fast. His early outings at PMQs were never less than competent, but there was an awkwardness to them, as if he were working out how to play the role of a man who had been elected leader of the Labour Party. But now we're beginning to see the real man. His questions are just as focused, but now there's an ability to think on his feet and to respond to the prime minister's lies and disinformation with genuine incredulity, anger and – when needed – humour. At PMQs there's only one person who looks fit to run the country, and it's not Boris.

Then again, it's not as if the Labour leader hasn't been spoiled for lines of attack on the prime minister, and predictably Starmer chose to go in on the exams chaos. Either Boris knew about the problem and chose to do nothing, or he didn't know about it when he should have done. Simple question: which one was it? Just as predictably, Boris resorted to bullshit and bluster. Labour had never wanted children to go back to school in the first place. An outright lie, as Starmer had unequivocally given his support to students returning on several occasions in May and June.

After that, Johnson had a full-on meltdown. Even the few Tories in the chamber had the grace to look embarrassed. First, Boris accused Keir of being anti-Brexit – as if having been a remainer meant you automatically wanted tens of thousands of people to die from the coronavirus and for the A-level results of less well-off students to be downgraded. He then went on to accuse Starmer of being an IRA supporter.

This was too much for both the Labour leader and the Speaker, Lindsay Hoyle. In the past, Hoyle has been reluctant to challenge Johnson when he goes off on a tangential mega-rant, but this time he was quick to rein him in. Starmer looked understandably furious and reminded Boris that as director of public prosecutions he had pressed charges against many terrorists. He could also have pointed out that it hadn't been him who had recently offered a peerage to Claire Fox, who defended the 1993 Warrington bombing when she was a member of the Revolutionary Communist Party.

'If he was a decent man, he would apologise,' Starmer said. But Boris isn't a decent man, so he didn't. Instead, he continued to rush on his run. There would be no extension to the furlough scheme because it would merely encourage people to hang around at home doing nothing. As if the prospect of being made unemployed was a lifestyle choice for millions of workers.

Starmer ended by asking why was Johnson now refusing to meet the families of those who had been bereaved by Covid-19, having promised to do so on TV just days earlier? Remind me, was this the twelfth or thirteenth U-turn in the past six weeks? Now was the time for Boris's sad face. Or failing that, serious face. But he can't do either, so he just smirked a little. The reason he wasn't going to see the bereaved wasn't because he cared too little but because he cared too much. Their stories might make him unhappy. And besides, it would be inappropriate as the bereaved were in litigation with the government. They weren't, but what's one more lie among so many?

The meltdown precipitated by Starmer continued for the rest of PMQs. Boris seemed to have no idea there were a huge number of industries, such as aviation, tourism and hospitality, that weren't going to return to normal anytime soon. Nor did he know that Matt Hancock had just extended some local lockdowns, at the very moment he was saying more people should be going back to work. One day, it might occur to Boris that some companies might not want to take a punt on their employees' health by forcing them back before the workplace is properly secure. But today wasn't that day. Rather, it was the day for Boris's carers to try to get him out of the Commons before he did any more damage to either the country or the Tory party.

It was also a day for those watching PMQs to ask themselves what they had done to deserve a leader who is visibly falling apart week on week. There was never anything very clever about Boris; now there isn't even anything funny. Of all the coronavirus joints in all the towns in the world he walks into ours.

* * *

The coronavirus wasn't the government's only problem. There was still Brexit to finalise, with the UK expected to have a new trade deal with the EU in place by the end of the year. So there was surprise and concern even among the most loyal of Tories when, in early September, Boris Johnson announced that he was planning on disapplying some sections of the Northern Ireland protocol on the movement of goods that he himself had negotiated with the EU just seven months previously. Threatening to break international laws and treaties – usually the stuff of rogue states – didn't strike many people as the best way of announcing that the UK was a trusted partner as it sought to agree new trade deals.

Brandon Lewis breaks cardinal law for MPs and tells the half-truth

8 SEPTEMBER 2020

Not even his most generous friends would describe Brandon Lewis as particularly bright. He is one of parliament's natural plodders. A born follower. A man who has unexpectedly found himself in the cabinet both by virtue of his more talented colleagues having disqualified themselves by being awkward and for having no principles of his own he could possibly compromise. But there seemed little harm in Boris Johnson promoting Brandon to Northern Ireland secretary once the Brexit withdrawal agreement and Northern Ireland protocol had been agreed in parliament last year, as there was little potential for him to screw up too badly.

That, though, was before the prime minister had, at the weekend, unilaterally declared that there were some bits of the Northern Ireland protocol he was unhappy with and planned to backtrack on. Which left Lewis with one of his more difficult and embarrassing hours as a minister as he struggled to answer an urgent question on the latest U-turn. By the end, both he and the government were in tatters.

It was something of an open goal for Louise Haigh, the shadow Northern Ireland secretary, but she gratefully accepted the opportunity with some style. Labour wanted Brexit to proceed on the terms the government had promised, with the protocol intact. And given that the government's chief legal adviser had resigned earlier that morning – civil servants have scruples about law-breaking, even if politicians don't – it rather looked as if Boris was planning to renege on his own treaty. One that he had drawn up himself, forced through parliament in under three days, and on which he had successfully fought a general election last December.

Now it appeared that the government had had second thoughts. That its treaty hadn't been an 'oven-ready' deal after all, and that it was planning to breach the ministerial code by breaking the law. Haigh even ended by quoting Margaret Thatcher, every Conservative MP's patron saint of conservatism: the UK did not renounce international treaties.

Beads of sweat began to appear on Lewis's forehead. He could sense he was in trouble; he just didn't know exactly how much, as he was far too insignificant to have been included in any of the decision-making. All he had been given was a one-paragraph brief telling him just to bluff it out as best he could for the duration of the urgent question. So he began to say any old nonsense that came into his head. Yes, Boris had had a bit of a brain freeze when he had negotiated the withdrawal agreement and it was a bit shit, but everyone was entitled to a bit of an off-day. The Brexit deal had never made complete sense, so it was only right that Boris should try to tie up a few loose ends by ignoring something that had been agreed by both the UK and the EU. But people shouldn't be too quick to pre-judge the situation. Just wait until Wednesday, when the government publishes its new get-out-of-jail internal market bill, and see if the EU is still complaining then. Clue: it would be. As would almost everyone else.

What followed was a near-universal pile-on from both sides of the house, with only Iain Duncan Smith, John Redwood and Steve Baker rushing to Lewis's defence. The kind of support Lewis could have done without as all three seemed to imply that Boris had promised them last year that he would renege on the Northern Ireland protocol, which was the only reason they had voted for it in the first place. Besides, it was vital that the UK could continue to offer state aid to tech companies, such as the one that had delivered the 'world-beating' test-and-trace coronavirus app. By the end, Lewis was all but begging them to shut up.

Theresa May was the first to go on the attack. The UK had signed the protocol, and it was our duty to abide by it. What would be the consequences for other international treaties if the UK could not be trusted to keep its word? We would be no better than any of the other failed rogue states the UK was always so quick to deplore for doing the same thing. Tory Simon Hoare made much the same point, as did a host of opposition MPs. Labour's

Hilary Benn wondered how the customs paperwork would operate under the proposed new regime. Lewis clearly didn't have a clue. By just throwing it in the bin? he shrugged.

Eventually, Brandon cracked. Asked yet again, this time by Tory Bob Neill, if the government was planning to break international law, Lewis made the schoolboy error of giving an almost honest response. Yes, of course we would be breaking the law, he snapped. But we would only be doing it in a little way and not so much that anyone would notice. It would be no worse than doing a little gentle recreational shoplifting after school. All shops priced a bit of pilfering into their balance sheet so there would be no harm done. It wasn't as if we were planning to nuke Brussels. Though Boris might like to keep that option on the table.

With this the floodgates opened. It was normal for ministers to lie at the dispatch box. MPs expected nothing else. So if Lewis had actually told a half-truth, then the reality must be even worse than they had thought. Was all this actually just a ploy to piss off the EU so much that we ended up saying 'Sod the Good Friday Agreement' and having a no-deal Brexit? Lewis opened and closed his mouth, but no words came out.

Ed Miliband revels in making Boris Johnson look like a second-rate con man

14 SEPTEMBER 2020

You could have been forgiven for imagining you were lost in a 2019 time warp: the House of Commons debating the Brexit withdrawal bill, nearly a year after that very bill had been passed. A bill that had been negotiated by the prime minister, declared an 'oven-ready' triumph by the prime minister, and with which he had won an 80-seat majority at the general election, after promising a despairing country that he would 'Get Brexit Done'.

On the plus side, though, we were treated to one of the best speeches of this and recent parliaments from Ed Miliband as he comprehensively ripped Boris Johnson's facile and fraudulent arguments to shreds. Admittedly, it wasn't the hardest of tasks, up against a man who can barely remember what he believed yesterday or even what excuses he might have made for his failures, but Miliband left Boris hopelessly exposed.

It wasn't immediately clear why Johnson had even made the last-minute decision to open the debate in person, as the business secretary, Alok Sharma, had originally been handed the poisoned chalice. And would probably have done a far better job, as Sharma has the unique talent of being able to put even himself to sleep whenever he opens his mouth. But perhaps hubris got the better of Boris. Or maybe he's just a common crook who can't resist returning to the scene of the crime. Either way, his guilt oozed from every pore.

This was Boris at his very worst. Normally, Johnson has little trouble in dealing in bullshit and lies; in fact, he has made a career out of it. Yet right from the very start, he appeared nervous and defensive, even though a near-empty chamber saved him from having to take too many embarrassing interventions from both the opposition and Conservative benches. Instead, what we got was total incoherence.

The EU wasn't negotiating in good faith. It was trying to blockade clotted cream being imported to Northern Ireland from Devon. The EU was trying to destroy the Northern Ireland protocol, and no British parliament could possibly sign up to this. Except, of course, it already had. Under his own leadership. Boris refused almost all interventions from the Labour benches, instead choosing to take those from the intellectually challenged Andrea Jenkyns and the timid rebel Bob Neill, who said he might be prepared to break international law, provided parliament was allowed a specific vote on it first. Boris happily indulged him in this nonsense.

Just one Tory, the former attorney general Jeremy Wright, challenged Boris on the ministerial code of breaking international law. Johnson ummed and ahed and said that Suella Braverman – a lawyer whom you wouldn't trust to witness a passport application and who had been chosen as attorney general for her compliance – had reckoned that the government could do anything Boris wanted it to. Wright – as with all the other former Tory attorney generals, prime ministers and cabinet ministers of any integrity – just shook his head in disbelief.

Under normal circumstances, the Labour leader would have replied for the opposition. But Keir Starmer was self-isolating after one of his children had displayed coronavirus symptoms, so Miliband, as shadow business secretary, got to make the speech he had originally prepared. And Miliband couldn't believe his luck, because many of his jibes might have fallen flat had they been levelled at Sharma. So much more fun to have the person actually responsible for trashing the reputation of both the country and the Conservative Party in front of you rather than a dull-witted apparatchik.

Miliband didn't put a foot wrong, both goading the prime minister for his failure to understand key aspects of the Northern Ireland protocol and enquiring how he expected other countries to take us at our word if we were so willing to break international treaties, before taking him down point by point. At first, Boris merely rolled his eyes, willing Ed to disappear, but by the end there was nothing but stone-cold fury in his stares. Boris has been found out countless times before by almost everyone who has had the misfortune to have dealings with him, but seldom so comprehensively and so publicly.

Or with such obvious enjoyment. Miliband knew he had Johnson bang to rights as a second-rate con man and wasn't going to let him off the hook. All his arguments were delivered with the panache and flourish of a man who knew he had right on his side. Even the Tories sensed it, with only Bernard Jenkin foolish enough to intervene on the prime minister's behalf. Miliband did for him in a couple of short sentences, saying that the Tory-led Northern Ireland select committee had reported that the EU had been negotiating in good faith.

What followed was one highlight after another. The serial incompetence of a man who couldn't remember it was his deal he was reneging on. The list of politicians who agreed that the deal had protected the Northern Ireland protocol. The observation that there already was a dispute resolution procedure that didn't involve the failed state option. But the collector's item was his invitation for Boris to back up his assertion that the withdrawal agreement imposed a blockade on GB goods into Northern Ireland.

'Come on,' Ed said, his voice laced with condescension. 'I know you're a details man. Show me the blockade. I will give way to you.' Boris remained almost immobile, the blood draining from his face. He was so, so busted. But Miliband wasn't finished. He also enjoyed himself with the five possible reasons for breaking the law. Especially the one about doing so in a specific and limited way. As if not going really big by actually invading Brussels and executing Michel Barnier somehow made it OK. He did, though, leave out a sixth reason: that Boris has yet to come across a law that ever applied to him.

The speeches that followed were something of an anticlimax in comparison. Bill Cash found that he could be even more angry now that Brexit was happening than when it wasn't, while SNP leader Ian Blackford attacked Johnson's proposals to remove powers from the devolved governments. Not that Boris was there to hear them. He had sneaked out of the chamber shortly after his evisceration. It turns out that Boris does have a humiliation threshold after all. And Miliband had just found it.

* * *

Throughout the summer it had felt as if the UK was slowly returning to normal. This feeling had been encouraged by the government, with such schemes as 'Eat Out to Help Out', whereby the Treasury would pick up £10 of the tab per person for anyone willing to go back out to eat in restaurants. But by the middle of September, it was clear that the easing in restrictions had been premature and that the rate of infections was again rising rapidly. On 14 September, Boris Johnson tried to counter this with the 'rule of six' – just six members of different households being allowed to meet up, whether indoors or outdoors – but this already felt like too little, too late. The R rate was well above 1, meaning the disease was spreading exponentially, and the first examples of the Kent variant were detected on 20 September. Two days later, there were nearly 5,000 new cases being detected daily. Johnson spoke of the need to avoid a second wave, seemingly unaware the country was already in the middle of it.

In 1940, we had Churchill; in 2020, we have Johnson's poundshop imitation

22 SEPTEMBER 2020

Some men are born mediocre. Some achieve mediocrity. Others have mediocrity thrust upon them. In 1940, we had Winston Churchill. In 2020, we have Boris Johnson, a man who believes himself to be Churchill's reincarnation, but is nothing more than a poundshop imitation.

Where to start with the prime minister's TV address to the nation? The trademark smirk? The nervous hand gestures? The fact he thinks he's fighting a war, not a pandemic? Or just the brazen cheek as Boris tried to claim the credit for what he called the stunning triumph over the coronavirus so far? The 50,000 dead and the endless screw-ups of his own government, from care homes to test and trace, were simply airbrushed out of history. The prime minister is not just a man without quality. He is a man without shame.

All this was just a warm-up for the grandiose announcement of a few extra restrictions that had already been announced and would almost certainly prove to be insufficient to cope with the second wave. Boris apologised for the new measures, though he laid the blame squarely on the British people for not having been able to abide by the existing measures. Perhaps he should have run that line past Dominic Cummings, who set an example so many followed.

'Never in our history has our collective destiny and our collective health depended so completely on our individual behaviour,' he said, winding up the Churchill rhetoric. 'There are unquestionably difficult months to come. And the fight against Covid is by no means over. I have no doubt, however, that there are great days ahead. But now is the time for us all to summon the discipline, and the resolve, and the spirit of togetherness that will carry us through.' Qualities that have yet to be found in Johnson.

It had been much the same story in the Commons earlier in the day, and you had to feel for Chris Whitty and Patrick Vallance, who must now be wondering why they had gone to so much trouble the previous day to explain just how critical the rates of coronavirus infection had become and that the threat had now risen back to level four. For, after a few token nods to the gravity of the situation – 'a stitch in time saves nine' – Boris used his Commons statement to introduce a few minor tweaks to lockdown restrictions that rather suggested he wasn't too bothered.

He wanted schools, colleges, universities and businesses to remain open – with the one proviso that all those he had previously threatened with the sack if they didn't go back to work were now advised to work from home, if at all possible. His biggest change was that pubs, restaurants and bars should now all close at 10 p.m. – it has apparently been proved that the coronavirus is mainly a nocturnal creature and is most contagious after dark – though people were obviously free to go home in groups of six, get totally hammered and infect one another afterwards.

Like most Johnson statements, it rather felt as if it had been written on the fly. By a committee of his left and right brain, with little synaptic contact between the two. There were few attempts to explain the situation carefully and carry the country with him. Just a load of off-the-cuff measures – mandatory face masks for shop and hospitality workers, etc. – and the threat of stricter measures to come if people didn't comply or the restrictions proved ineffective.

This time he was really, really serious, he said, trying not to smirk. He understood that, unlike the Hun, we Brits were too freedom-loving to comply with every law – nothing to do with the government's mixed messaging, obviously – but there were limits. There was nothing the public liked less than one law for the powerful and another for everyone else, so unless it involved driving up to Durham for eye tests, it was time to rein in our libertarian instincts.

These restrictions could last for up to six months, Boris added. Which immediately raised eyebrows on both sides of the Commons. Because the prime minister's idea of time rarely coincides with anyone else's. It was Boris who had initially said the worst of the pandemic would be over in 12 weeks. It was Boris who had said we should be back to normal by Christmas. Now he was saying we were in for another half-year. Which meant that you could probably double it. Maybe he was thinking of Christmas 2021.

The pandemic has highlighted the stark difference between Boristime and Coronatime. Because he is unable to treat the country as grown-ups and can't handle being the bearer of bad news, Boris invariably shortens any given Covid time frame. Years become months, months become weeks. You sometimes can't even tell if one of his promises is going to last till the end of a sentence. Meanwhile, Coronatime has the last laugh by turning each of his strategies from weeks into months and days into weeks.

If Keir Starmer was put out that his powerful virtual conference speech had been all but forgotten by lunchtime, he showed no sign of it. Rather, he maintained his familiar tactic of broadly supporting the government's new measures, before pointing out some of their more obvious shortcomings. Were there any signs that localised lockdowns were proving effective? What financial support was Boris planning to offer for jobs and businesses affected by the new restrictions? And whatever had happened to the world-beating test-and-trace system that everyone had agreed was essential to containing the virus?

Mostly, though, Boris's concentration was focused on keeping his own backbenchers happy, as half of them want to avoid any further restrictions to keep the economy open and half have genuine concerns that the party will not be forgiven if the death toll in the second wave matches or exceeds that of the first. And by and large he succeeded in treading an uneasy balance between being too bullish and too pragmatic. Up until the end, that is. Then his natural enthusiasm got the better of him. The ludicrous £100 billion Operation Moonshot was still on course, and with any luck everything would be fine within a matter of a few months.

We were back on Boristime. Though not for long, as moments after he had finished speaking Nicola Sturgeon made her own statement to the Scottish parliament. Where Boris had sounded somewhat rambling and, at times, contradictory in his statement, Nicola was a model of clarity and precision. She has a clear grasp of her priorities and sticks to them. She had listened to the advice of Whitty and Vallance and concluded it was necessary to go a lot further than England had. In Scotland, the rule of six was a goner, and there would be no unnecessary socialising between families indoors for the foreseeable future.

With Northern Ireland having already reached a similar conclusion, that left Boris as something of an outlier. Already people were taking bets that his new restrictions would have to be updated within a week. In the battle between Boristime and Coronatime, there's so far only ever been one winner.

Boris Johnson's latest Covid strategy: no hope and no end in sight

12 OCTOBER 2020

History repeats itself. Sort of. There are now more people in hospital with coronavirus than there were in March, when the prime minister imposed a lockdown on the entire country. The difference back then was that those restrictions came with the promise of some kind of strategy: measures to reduce the pressures on the NHS while an effective local track-and-trace system could be introduced that would allow targeted lockdowns where necessary.

Six months on, with countless broken promises on testing targets, including the deranged Operation Moonshot and a track-and-trace system clearly unfit for purpose, Boris Johnson was back in the Commons to announce a new plan for the country. Only this one came with no end in sight. There was no glimmer of hope; just an exhortation to keep aimlessly buggering on. The only upside was that if you did get Covid-19, then you were less likely to die of it than before, as hospitals had become better at treating it. Unless the hospitals got completely overloaded. Then it was back to as you were.

Johnson looked knackered before he even started, his complexion even more pallid than usual and his eyes mere pinpricks. For a moment it looked as if the narcissist had been confronted with his own sense of futility. A situation that he couldn't bend to his will, no matter how delusional the thought process. He is cornered by hubris, a man hating every second of his life but condemned to experience its unforgiving horror. Not even the health secretary could be bothered to attend to watch this latest meltdown.

'We have taken a balanced approach,' Johnson began. As in, he was too slow to react back in March, with the result that the government has presided over one of the world's highest death tolls. As in, he did next to nothing during the summer, when we had a chance to prepare for autumn. As in, for weeks he actively encouraged people to go back to work, before switching to advise them against it. As in, unlocking the north at the same time as the south, even though infection rates in the north remained higher. That kind of balanced.

What Boris had to offer now was a new three-tiered approach: 'bad', 'very bad' and 'very, very bad'. 'Bad' would apply to most of the country and would involve people doing pretty much what they had been doing for the last couple of months. Rule of six and all that. 'Very bad' would mean that those areas that had already been under the more stringent lockdown restrictions would remain so, though if you wanted to meet a few friends outdoors in the garden for a beer to let each other know how depressed you were feeling, you now could. And 'very, very bad' meant that you could only see your mates if you happened to be in the pub at the same time and ordered five Cornish pasties to go with your bottle of Scotch.

It was all verifiably a bit nuts. Because as of yet the government has no scientific evidence that the hospitality industry is the prime source of infection, so it could all have been a waste of time. Because the government was in a fight with local leaders from around the country as to which tier they should be in: so far only Merseyside is classified as 'very, very bad', and London's mayor, Sadiq Khan, was pushing for London to be upgraded within days. Because local areas were economically better off if classified as 'very bad'. Mostly because the R rate was between 1.2 and 1.5 nationally, so the virus was going to continue to spread whatever happened.

Often in the past, Keir Starmer has been unequivocal in his support for the government's coronavirus measures. This time, he was rather more circumspect. Mostly because it was hard to see how much difference the new measures were going to make, other than to relabel every area of the country, but partly because there are a lot of Labour MPs who fear for the economies of their constituencies and are keen to be downgraded as far as possible. Not to mention those MPs who didn't trust the government to know where their constituencies actually were and to wrongly classify them. For Boris, anything further north than Islington is the wilderness.

It was no surprise that most other opposition MPs were sceptical, wondering whether stopping community transmission and an effective test-and-trace system would have been of more value, but what was most striking was how few Tory MPs were wholehearted in their enthusiasm. Some because they believe that any restriction on an Englishman's liberty should be resisted – if you die, you die, get over it – but most because they too have no faith in Boris. The loss of trust in the prime minister is more contagious than the pandemic. It's slowly dawned on them that he really is just fumbling around in the dark.

Boris still had to endure a Downing Street press conference, where he was called on to repeat much of what he had said in the Commons. Though this time he had Rishi Sunak and Chris Whitty to offer a limited helping hand; the chief medical officer's most uplifting message was that things could easily have been a great deal worse and that the restrictions in all tiers would have to become more severe to be effective. Which rather undermined most of what the prime minister had been saying.

Johnson did his best to retrieve the situation with the vague hope that things might be a bit better by Christmas. But even the eternal optimist didn't sound confident. Boris had intended his new simplified guidelines to be reassuring. To let the country feel he had the situation in hand. Yet all he had really achieved was to remind everyone that he was out of his depth and had no real answers to anything. Like all of us, he was just dancing in the dark. Beam me up, Whitty.

Boris falls into Keir's tiers trap and goes full delusional over TfL

21 OCTOBER 2020

It wouldn't be prime minister's questions without Boris Johnson being accused of telling at least one lie. Indeed, in recent months it has often felt as if Boris has taken a bet with Dominic Cummings to see if he can outdo himself on the lies of the week before. But normally Boris saves his biggest fibs for his exchanges with Keir Starmer. This time, he reserved his top Trumps for London MPs concerned about planned changes to Transport for London and the council tax.

Not that Starmer didn't yet again comfortably get the better of Johnson; rather, he seemed to have grown tired of a full-on assault on the prime minister and decided to employ simple logic in an effort to get Boris to commit himself to something he might later regret. And in that he was extremely effective. Because it will be in only about a month's time that Johnson will realise just how much trouble he has unwittingly got himself into. Though whether he will care is another matter. Like all narcissists, Boris lives only for the moment.

The Labour leader opened with a simple question: how does a region that gets put into tier 3 ever get out of it? Simple, said Boris. When the rate of infection falls below 1. Fine, Starmer replied. Except that on current evidence there was no sign of the R rate falling below 1 any time soon. Only Cornwall and possibly the Isle of Wight currently had an infection rate lower than Manchester when it was in effect put into tier 2 back in July. And we all knew where Manchester was now.

What's more, there were no guarantees those regions that had been put into tier 3 would be much better off than they had been before. Even the chief medical officer and the chief scientific adviser had said tier 3 restrictions wouldn't be enough to lower the rate of infection. And as it had been proved already that almost every tier 2 region would inevitably end up in tier 3, the government was merely piling on months of agony, with no exit plan.

This was the kind of straightforward logic that invariably defeats Johnson, and his telltale bullshit tics kicked in: the shouting, the waving of arms and the needy glances towards his own benches. 'Um . . .' said Boris. He was reviewing each region every 28 days. Before keeping it precisely where it was. Why else would he have been negotiating a six-month deal for Manchester if he had imagined there was a cat in hell's chance of the region having its restrictions eased before then?

'Ah, Manchester,' Starmer segued easily. The prime minister who could waste £40 million on a non-existent garden bridge and spend £6,000 a day on test-and-trace consultants didn't seem to be able to find £5 million for Manchester. Nonsense, Boris blustered. The Tories were one-nation Conservatives who brought the country together by pitting one council against another. Labour merely wanted to close everything down with a circuit break for months on end. Aka two to three weeks. At this Starmer zoned out. History would prove one of them right within a couple of months. And he was totally confident he would be history's chosen one. Sometimes it paid to play the long game.

Relieved to have got off more lightly than he expected – spotting trouble coming down the track has never been his strong point – Boris went full delusional when challenged by three Labour London MPs and one Tory about the proposed shake-up of Transport for London and the responsibilities of Sadiq Khan, the London mayor. It was worse than listening to a child explaining how the dog ate his homework. Cringe-worthy.

It was also telling just how personal Johnson's hatred for Khan is. He can't stand the fact that Sadiq is more popular in London than him, nor can he bear it that Khan has unarguably done a better job than he did as London mayor. So Boris went into hissy-fit overdrive, where one lie was immediately topped by another. Sadiq had bankrupted the city, he was personally responsible for the damage to Hammersmith Bridge – at least when your own bridge is only in your imagination you can't do any damage to it – and Londoners deserved everything that was coming down the road to make their lives more miserable for having backed him.

None of which was true. According to TfL's accounts, since Khan took over from Johnson in 2016 he has reduced the deficit by 71% and increased cash reserves by 16%. That TfL is now in trouble is entirely down to the pandemic. Not even Johnson's own MPs could stomach these lies. Asking for the country's trust during a national crisis when you can't even tell the truth about an audited balance sheet is an uphill struggle. If the prime minister will lie about this, what won't he lie about?

Still, though, Johnson wasn't finished. Before the opposition day debate on Marcus Rashford's proposals to extend free school meals throughout the holidays up until Easter, Boris was twice asked to take the proposals seriously. Twice he declined. The thing about children that he had just discovered was that they didn't actually need to eat during school holidays. Their metabolisms stopped. And besides, going hungry was the kind of character-building quality that the country would need in a post-Brexit, post-Covid world. It was as crass as it was tin-eared. Johnson has already caved in to Rashford once, and the chances are that sometime soon he will be forced to do so again. But when you are programmed to have all failures expunged from your memory, these are the kinds of mistakes you make.

* * *

The report into anti-Semitism in the Labour Party was more damning than expected. As well as finding the Labour leadership guilty of political interference in the handling of complaints, the Equality and Human Rights Commission found specific examples of harassment and discrimination. Jeremy Corbyn, the former leader, refused to accept the findings of the EHRC in full and was suspended from the Labour Party by Keir Starmer.

Meanwhile, Johnson was still dithering over what to do about the second wave of Covid. SAGE had privately recommended that the country needed a four-week lock-down – a circuit-breaker to reduce the transmission of the disease – back in September, but Boris had overruled the scientists. Maintaining a feel-good mentality and preserving the economy were deemed more important than protecting the nation's health. But by the end of October, Johnson was unable to ignore the evidence and was forced to introduce a four-week lockdown. Something that was widely seen as too little, too late.

Subdued Johnson just a piece of flotsam being buffeted around

2 NOVEMBER 2020

Looking on the bright side for the prime minister, he didn't have any more credibility to lose. As a rule of thumb, you can pretty much guarantee that for everything that Boris Johnson says, the opposite will turn out to be true.

As with Brexit, so it is for the coronavirus. In March, he insisted the virus would be defeated in 12 weeks. That went well. In July, Boris promised the country would be back to normal by Christmas. No one's putting any money on that now. In his statement to the Commons on the latest national lockdown, Johnson insisted the virus would be beaten by March. He didn't say what year.

It's hard to know which is the more bewildering: the fact that we have a prime minister who is both incompetent and unable to distinguish between fact and fiction; or that there are so many Conservative MPs who are consistently taken aback by the failings of their leader. You would have thought by now it would have been 203 times bitten, 204 times shy. But no. They continue to cut him some slack, albeit increasingly grumpily, as if they are as surprised as anyone that Johnson has failed to deliver on his promises, and each time insist he is now on a final warning. Something has to change, they warn. But it never does.

Johnson was in the Commons to give the statement he had already been forced to give at Saturday's Downing Street press conference after details of the national lockdown agreed between him, Rishi Sunak, Michael Gove and Matt Hancock had been mysteriously leaked to the papers the night before. Not that it was a national lockdown, mind, because Boris had promised there would not be another national lockdown. Rather it was a lockdown that would be imposed nationally, albeit with schools and universities remaining more or less open.

This was a subdued Boris. Even by his own standards, this latest U-turn was a humiliation. An admission that he has not just lost control of the coronavirus, he's lost control of the government. He's just a piece of flotsam being buffeted around. Not that it stopped him lying, of course. Just that the lies have become progressively more feeble, as if even he has stopped the pretence of believing them.

He began by stating that the government had had to change course because the scientific data had changed on Saturday. The chief scientific adviser and chief medical officer had actually given their latest briefing to the cabinet well before that, which was why the lockdown had been agreed on Friday. SAGE had called for a 'circuit-breaker' back in September and had been clear a tiered series of regional lockdowns was going to be insufficient to contain the spread of the virus.

But Boris didn't want to upset his more libertarian MPs, so he decided to kill a few more people instead.

Besides, it would have been shameless opportunism to introduce a lockdown any sooner.

For weeks now, Johnson has been dismissively referring to Keir Starmer as Captain Hindsight. Now he was tacitly forced to admit that the Labour leader was Captain Foresight and he was General Hopelessness. Because the measures that Boris was introducing were ones which Starmer had been demanding for the best part of a month. Something which Keir was not slow to point out. The new lockdown was both harder and longer than the one Labour had proposed and less likely to succeed.

With Labour having promised Johnson the necessary votes on Wednesday, most of the rest of the session was a free-for-all, with the prime minister as the fall guy. A lot of the flak came as friendly fire. Tory Brexiters hadn't fought to close borders only to curtail every Englishman's right to go into any pub they wanted to get Covid-19.

Just as long as the virus wasn't caught from Johnny Foreigner, then all was tickety-boo. You could die happy knowing the virus had spread from a Brit. Why bother flying to Zurich, when you can turn the whole of the UK into a Dignitas hub? Who knows, it could turn out to be a huge money-spinner.

The longer the session went on, the more confused Johnson's answers became. He was adamant the country would return to regional lockdowns on 2 December, even though he could give no guarantees the rate of infection would have come down sufficiently over the course of the next month. He guessed it would be down to parliament what happened next, he said unhappily. So that was a 'yes' and a 'no'.

'The country wants politicians to act together,' he shrugged sadly, apparently unaware of his own failure to act on scientific evidence and work with Labour a month ago – and of the fact that the MPs least inclined to work together were his own. Some wanted golf courses reopened; others were happy to compromise on pitch and putt. The DUP's Sammy Wilson said that he had come to hear Churchill, but had got only Halifax-style appeasement instead.

What became more and more evident the longer the session went on was that Boris was out of ideas. Other than to do too little, too late. He wasn't even sure what he had and hadn't promised Scotland by way of a bailout. Starmer slumped back in his seat. He knew what we all knew: that we would be back in the Commons on 2 December, with little change in the nation's health, to have the same arguments over lockdowns and the failure of test and trace all over again. You can cancel Christmas now.

* * *

Over in the US, the presidential election had taken place on 3 November. The race between President Trump and Joe Biden for the White House had always been predicted to be close, and early results showed the two candidates to be neck-and-neck. But due to the pandemic there were many more postal votes cast in this election than in previous ones, so counting was delayed, with some of the key swing states late in completing their counts. These states proved to be decisive in a Biden victory that wasn't declared until three and a half days after the election. Predictably, Trump wasn't going to go quietly, alleging widespread voter fraud in all the close counts he had lost. Curiously, he never for a moment suspected malpractice in the states he had narrowly won. The attorney general later declared there had been no irregularities, but still the Donald and his supporters refused to accept this. To this day, Trump insists the election was stolen from him, and he was in too much of a sulk to attend Biden's inauguration in January 2021.

PM channels his inner John Wayne in vaccine metaphor meltdown

9 NOVEMBER 2020

Shortly before 5 p.m. in the UK, President-elect Joe Biden gave a press conference. The results of the trials were very promising, he said, but there was still a long way to go before a vaccination programme could be rolled out nationwide. So it was now more important than ever not to let your guard down and to carry on wearing masks. It was coherent, informative, and in less than five minutes Biden had told Americans just about everything they needed to know.

Boris Johnson likes to do things rather differently. Almost to the second after Biden had finished speaking, the prime minister stepped out into the Downing Street briefing room, flanked by the deputy chief medical officer, Jonathan Van-Tam, and Brigadier Joe Fossey, dressed in full camo gear that had the reverse effect of drawing attention to himself. A new form of anti-camo perhaps.

After a few introductions, Boris went on one of his long rambles. He didn't really have anything to say that couldn't have been wrapped up in minutes, but he considers a press conference not to have taken place unless he's wasted the best part of an hour of everyone's time.

Perhaps it was the excitement of having a real-life soldier standing next to him, but Johnson's explanation of the new vaccination trials was relayed in a series of metaphors straight out of the movie *Stagecoach*. The arrows were in the quiver! The cavalry was on its way; the toot of the bugle – Michael Gove's presumably – was getting louder but still some way off. Having a prime minister who manages to trivialise something really important is getting extremely draining and it's hard not to zone out within moments of him starting a sentence. So much for the great communicator.

Next up was the brigadier, who is in charge of the mass testing in Liverpool and looked uncomfortable throughout. 'Two thousand troops have answered the call,' he said, making it sound as if the soldiers had had some say in their deployment rather than been told they were off to Liverpool for the next four weeks. He then pulled out a piece of plastic from his pocket. 'You know what a swab is,' he continued. 'Well, this is the lateral flow that gives you a result within an hour.' And that was all he had to say. He didn't seem at all sure what the lateral flow actually was or how it worked, but then he was only following orders. If he'd had his way, he'd have saved the taxpayer a return train ticket from Liverpool to London.

There was no slide show this time – obviously No. 10 has started to wonder if they are more trouble than they are worth after recent events – so Van-Tam was left to ad-lib on the vaccine trial. Even though he had no more information than Boris, so all he could do was repeat the fact that it was exciting, but we shouldn't get carried away just yet. Try to think of it as a penalty shootout, he said – Boris's crap analogies are as contagious as the coronavirus. We've scored the first goal, so we know the keeper can be beaten, but there was a long way to go before the match was won. No one seemed to have told Van-Tam that the expectation in a shootout was that the penalty-taker would score.

Things carried on in much the same vein when questions came in from the media. The brigadier tried to make himself as inconspicuous as possible – merging into the background was part of his SAS training – and so the only other thing he had to offer was that he was just on day four of his deployment, so it was hard to tell whether things were going well or badly. Van-Tam desperately hunted around for new ways of saying the vaccination trials were still at an early stage, but things were looking more hopeful for next year.

Try to think of yourself as being in a railway station on a wet and windy night, he said, doing his best to channel his inner Fat Controller. You could see the lights of the train two miles away. Then the train pulled into the station, and you didn't know if the door was going to open. Next, you couldn't even be sure whether there would be enough seats for everyone. The UK had only ordered enough vaccines for about a third of the population, so unless more doses came online, most people were going to miss out. It didn't sound quite as hopeful as he had suggested. But maybe that's just the way he tells them.

Boris, meanwhile, just looked relieved to only get one question on the US presidential election. And that wasn't even on if he had spoken to the president-elect – he hadn't, as Biden has been too busy taking calls from Micronesia – or if he had any reaction to being called a 'shape-shifting creep' by a former adviser to Barack Obama. The Democrats still haven't forgiven Boris for his remarks about Obama's part-Kenyan ancestry giving him a dislike of the British Empire.

'I congratulate the president-elect,' said Johnson, sidestepping a suggestion he give Donald Trump a call to persuade him to throw in the towel. The US and the UK had had a close relationship in the past and no doubt would in the future. He had nothing to say on Brexit. Rather, he chose to accentuate the shared climate change objectives of COP27. Or COP26, as the rest of the world knows it.

* * *

When Boris Johnson became prime minister in July 2020, he had installed two of the old Vote Leave team in key Downing Street positions: Lee Cain as communications director and Dominic Cummings as chief adviser. Both had appeared safe in their roles – indeed, there were many in Westminster who thought they were virtually running the government – and yet over the course of a couple of days in mid-November both men were gone. You can take your pick as to whether they resigned or were sacked, as their departures were shrouded in mystery. One version had it that Cain had been offered a promotion, which he had refused, choosing to leave instead, and that Cummings had always intended to leave No. 10 by the end of the year. This version ended with all three men having a nice farewell laugh together and Boris Johnson giving Cain a pair of boxing gloves with 'Get Brexit Done' written on them.

Other sources suggested that there had been a power struggle in No. 10 between Cummings, Cain and the prime minister's partner, Carrie Symonds – allegedly nicknamed Princess Nut Nuts by Cain and Cummings – over the direction of the government. The Symonds camp, strengthened by the appointment of Allegra Stratton as Johnson's new spokesperson, believed that a new, cuddlier, less combative approach was needed during the pandemic. What we do know is that Cummings was seen scuttling out of the front door of Downing Street carrying a cardboard box full of papers and a few days later wrote a newspaper article criticising Boris for being indecisive. The full fallout of Cummings's removal from No. 10 would take months – perhaps years – to become clear.

Elsewhere in Westminster, Keir Starmer decided to readmit Jeremy Corbyn to the Labour Party, after the former leader insisted that he had not said that anti-Semitism within the party had been overstated. On 19 November, the Cabinet Office published a report that found that home secretary Priti Patel had been guilty of breaking the ministerial code by bullying colleagues. In normal times, such a damning verdict would have been a sackable offence, but Johnson merely chose to ignore the report. Presumably because Patel bullied him into not firing her.

Tiers of a clown as Boris Johnson's video link falls down

23 NOVEMBER 2020

On a normal Monday the Commons might have been preoccupied with the prime minister's 'unintentional' decision not to sack Priti Patel, after she was found guilty of having broken the ministerial code on bullying. Instead, the home secretary's behaviour was long forgotten, as Boris Johnson used the time to announce the new coronavirus measures instead.

Talking via a video link from No. 10, where he is still self-isolating, Johnson said we were returning to the tiered system, which worked so well the first time that a second lockdown became a necessity. Though these new tiers would be quite different from the old tiers. In some ways they would be more relaxed, with non-necessary retail and gyms now allowed to open in all levels. And in tiers 1 and 2, some outdoor and indoor spectators would be allowed to attend sporting events, while in tier 2 no one would be allowed into a pub unless they also ordered a substantial meal. Go figure. Tier 3 would be more or less like the current national lockdown, apart from the bits that wouldn't. It all felt pretty much like something that had been cobbled together on the back of a fag packet in cabinet to fit in with what the libertarian wing of the Tory party might accept, rather than something that was based on hard scientific evidence.

But Boris didn't want us to feel too gloomy about everything. The vaccine trials did look promising, testing was improving, and all being well we might be back to more or less normal by Easter. And as a special treat – though he couldn't yet go into exact details – there would be some kind of amnesty over Christmas so families could meet up. Though this had to kept hush-hush for now, because if the coronavirus got wind of any relaxations in measures, it could seek to take advantage by working overtime and leaving many elderly relatives dead in January and February. There again, it's been a long old year for Covid-19 as well, so maybe the virus could do with a four-day break too.

Keir Starmer didn't sound wholly convinced. He's heard too many broken promises from Johnson already and, having backed the government on all its previous public health measures, he wanted a little more detail on the package before conferring his blessing. How confident was Johnson that these new tiers weren't also going to end up in another lockdown? And when would he announce which regions would be put into which tiers? There were going to be some mightily pissed-off people in the north of England if they were to find themselves back in tier 3, if parts of London and the south-east – where the R rate was at its highest – remained in tier 2. As an aside, Starmer ended by saying the government had rather forgotten the 'track' and 'isolate' bits of test, track and isolate.

But this was Boris at his most nonchalant. His answers to the Labour leader amounted to little more than qualified thanks for the opposition's support, and he again gave the chamber the distinct impression that he was more interested in coming up with a system of measures that all of his own party could tolerate, rather than one designed to beat the virus. Something that was borne out in his reply to Mark Harper, who declared he and his fellow Conservative MP Steve Baker had written to the prime minister demanding evidence for his policies. This felt like trying to get a parent to prove the existence of Santa, though Baker demanding policy-driven evidence was a first for the MP for Wycombe. Next, the Brexiter will be threatening to go to the European Court of Human Rights. Oh. He already has. The irony was not lost on anyone.

At which point the sound link from No. 10 went down. 'Have you muted yourself?' said the Speaker, Lindsay Hoyle, hopefully. 'Have you pressed the button?' Still nothing. Boris's IT skills don't appear to have been noticeably improved by his lessons from Jennifer Arcuri.

Just as Hoyle was about to suspend the session, amid much laughter, you could hear Johnson plaintively yell: 'Some problem with the sound.' But the Speaker had heard too much already and handed over the next 45 minutes of the session to Matt Hancock to answer the questions, as he reckoned we'd more likely hear more sense.

Not that the health secretary had any better answers than Boris, but at least his smirk looks more serious as he gives his non-committal answers than the prime minister's. There was an understandable edge of panic in Door Matt's voice. Not just at being unexpectedly put on the spot, but out of an awareness that the latest measures are guesswork just as much as the previous ones.

Shortly after 5 p.m. we did get Johnson back, seemingly from another room in No. 10 that had been hastily converted into a new comms nerve centre, aka somewhere you could operate the broadband connection via a personal hotspot. But we didn't really learn anything new.

It looked as if Boris was still experiencing IT problems a couple of hours later, when he left the chief medical officer for England, Chris Whitty, and Andrew Pollard, director of the Oxford Vaccine Group, waiting at their Downing Street lecterns like a couple of spare parts as he failed to show up on his remote screen. But eventually the prime minister managed to reboot his laptop for a press conference that was basically a rerun of his Commons statement, albeit with more focus on the vaccine.

Johnson happily went into a string of lazy metaphors – 'the drumming hooves of the cavalry coming over the hill', ''tis the season to be jolly, but also the season to be jolly careful' – before lapsing into rhyme with 'squeeze the disease'.

Not for the first time, it was left to the scientists to remind everyone to basically ignore the prime minister and listen to them instead.

Major Sulk enters his darkest hour as rank and file desert him

1 DECEMBER 2020

Out of desperation more than anything else, Boris Johnson has taken to calling Keir Starmer Captain Hindsight. Even when the Labour leader is making predictions about what will happen next. But in the Commons debate on the new coronavirus tiers, the prime minister revealed a new persona for himself: Major Sulk.

You could tell Johnson wasn't a happy bunny from the off, because he arrived looking a total mess. More often than not, Boris's appearance is less art than artifice. He hopes that appearing shambolic will make people think he's not too bothered. That he's the Mr Good-Time Guy on whom you can rely for a joke. Except no one is laughing any more. Least of all Boris. His bedraggled, slumped demeanour was not a sign that he wasn't bothered. Rather, it was the opposite. He couldn't bear for his public to see just how much he did care. Not for the country, obviously. But for himself.

Up till now, the Great Narcissistic Sulk has never really

given a toss about his rank-and-file backbenchers. He didn't even know the names of three-quarters of them. But this was the day he came to realise the one-way love affair was over and the magic had worn off for a significant number of the Conservative parliamentary party. MPs willing to give him the benefit of the doubt because he had managed to win an 80-seat majority now realised they had bought a dud. A prime minister who at a time of crisis could be relied on to let you down.

Johnson's opening speech was a lazy, badly argued ramble through the familiar arguments he had been making over the past week. He began by listing the positives of the new regime – hairdressers, gyms and round-the-clock shopping – insisting that the evidence for reopening them had been taken with granular thoroughness. Despite the fact that his economic impact assessments, released at the last minute the previous day, bore a closer resemblance to something knocked up on the back of a cigarette packet.

He then went on to say that no one should take Christmas for granted. Only that was precisely what he was doing by granting a five-day Christmas amnesty that could turn into a New Year killing zone. He also promised an extra £1,000 to every pub that didn't serve Scotch eggs as a sop to the Tory malcontents. Or beer money, as Starmer scathingly described it. The longer Boris spoke, the emptier his words became. By the end, he was running on fumes.

In reply, the Labour leader merely voiced what was on everyone's mind. We'd all been here before on several occasions with Johnson, but every time he had let the country down. He had been too late to lock down initially; he had ignored SAGE's advice for a circuit-breaker in September; he had introduced a tiering system that was soon proved to be hopelessly inadequate; Typhoid Dido's track and trace had been a joke. He had promised the pandemic would be over by the summer. And then by Christmas.

Now we were clinging on for dear life, waiting for the vaccines to save us. So why should anyone believe a word the prime minister said, when it looked as though the new tiers were guided by what Boris could smuggle past enough of his backbenchers rather than by the science? A third national lockdown in January was all but an inevitability. And in the meantime, where was the financial help for the hospitality sector and the self-employed? As so often, Johnson had over-promised and under-delivered.

Even so, something had to be better than nothing. So Labour would be abstaining to make sure everyone's main focus was on the number of Tory rebels. Yet again, then, Starmer would be giving Johnson the benefit of the doubt and putting the government on notice. It's been on notice for a while now. There would come a time when Keir would have to say enough was enough and vote against the government on its handling of the coronavirus. But now was not the right time.

The rest of the debate was dominated by unhappy Tories either promising to rebel or to vote reluctantly for the government. Bernard Jenkin, after listing all the many faults in the new tiering system, sadly concluded that he would vote for Boris. Out of pity as much as anything else. Others were less forgiving, demanding more localised banding of tiers and proof that the hospitality industry was the root of all Covid evils. Steve Baker even went so far as to demand expert evidence. This from the MP who happily ignored both experts and evidence during numerous Brexit debates. Better a sinner who repenteth, I suppose.

It was Chris Grayling who delivered the real *coup de grâce* by saying that he was 'very concerned'. When you've lost the trust of Failing Grayling, who has cost the taxpayer more than £3 billion in a ministerial career of unrivalled uselessness, then you've lost the soul of the Tory party.

With Labour abstaining, the vote itself was a formality, the motion passing with a majority of 213. But with 56 Tories voting against him and more abstaining, this was Boris's darkest hour. One from which he may never recover. Many of us saw through Johnson long ago. An opportunist chancer interested only in self-glorification. Now it looks as if the mist has lifted from the eyes of many on his own benches. Enough for him to never again take a vote for granted. What goes around, comes around.

Man-child Gavin Williamson plumbs new depths of stupidity

3 DECEMBER 2020

Much to everyone's surprise, we have learned that Boris Johnson can – just occasionally – engage his brain before speaking. Having begun the Wednesday-night Downing Street press briefing with his usual mangled militaristic and jingoistic metaphors about 'the searchlights of science' and Britain having pioneered vaccination in the 18th century, he actually twice refrained from saying that Brexit was responsible for the UK being the first country to license the Pfizer/BioNTech vaccine. Just imagine: a prime minister known for being a lying, opportunistic chancer actually decided to tell the truth for once.

Would that the same could be said for some of his cabinet colleagues. Only on Wednesday, Matt Hancock and Jacob Rees-Mogg had described the vaccine as a Brexit bonus. On Thursday, Gavin Williamson, the education secretary man-child who has yet to move up to secondary-school level and whose career since winning fireplace salesman of the year two years running in 2006 and 2007 has been a mystery to us all, ratcheted up the nationalism to a new level. Asked by LBC's Nick Ferrari if Brexit had meant that the UK had got the vaccine ahead of the EU and the US, Gav went rogue.

'Well, I just reckon we've got the very best people in this country,' he said, 'and we've obviously got the best medical regulator, much better than the French have, much better than the Belgians have, much better than the Americans have. That doesn't surprise me at all because we're a much better country than every single one of them.' Even for Gav – the man who, before he was sacked as the Private Pike defence secretary for leaking National Security Council briefings, had said in response to the Salisbury poisonings that 'Russia should shut up and go away' – this was well out there.

Just think about the level of stupidity for a moment. Not only does Williamson have no first-hand knowledge of other countries' medical regulators – don't forget he is also the education secretary who failed to spot in March that the coronavirus pandemic would have knock-on consequences, with the cancellation of school exams – he is seemingly unaware that Pfizer is a US company and that the vaccine is being produced in Belgium.

Quite apart from a willingness to casually insult the rest of the world for being more crap than the UK – one day Gav might like to compare global coronavirus death rates – he had singled out two countries that were at the forefront of the development of vaccines. It was much like saying that Britain was now in the lead in the space race because we have Tim Peake.

You'd have thought that Williamson might have wanted to cut his losses at that point and tried to steer the conversation back to his department's plans to make exams easier next year. Or, failing that, its plans to admit girls to Eton – something that might have led to some unwanted pregnancies in Boris's time. But he carried on regardless, ignoring his special adviser, who must have been making frantic throat-cutting gestures in the corner of the room. Asked again if he was actually saying that Brexit had given the UK an advantage, he continued digging. 'I think just being able to get on with things,' he said, 'deliver it and the brilliant people in our medical regulator making it happen, means that people in this country are going to be the first in the western world – in the world – to get that Pfizer vaccine.'

As if the rest of the world was on a deliberate go-slow, bogged down in pointless bureaucracy to deny their people the vaccine. One day it may dawn on him that the race to find a vaccine has been a global effort. You have to wonder what *kompromat* Gav has on the prime minister for him to somehow still remain a cabinet minister.

Thank God, then, for England's deputy chief medical officer, Jonathan Van-Tam, the breakout star of the government's team of scientific advisers who had been sent out to do all the morning media rounds, on the grounds that he was just about the only person in the country the public trusted for independent advice. Talking on *BBC Breakfast* and Radio 5 Live, he immediately trashed Williamson by saying no one should read anything much into the Medicines and Healthcare products Regulatory

Agency being the first to license the vaccine. Other countries were also working round the clock, and he expected some of them to give their approval long before a needle had been jabbed into any Brit's arm.

JVT – as he's come to be known – gave similarly measured responses to other questions. The vaccine was our equaliser in the 70th minute – he can't resist a football or train analogy. No, it hadn't been fully tested on pregnant women, people over 50 were being prioritised because they accounted for 99% of all coronavirus deaths, the AstraZeneca results were looking promising as none of those who had been given the vaccine had been hospitalised, and the long-term aim was for as many people as possible to be vaccinated to relieve pressure on the NHS and reduce infection rates.

And he was sure the MHRA was working as fast as possible on approving other vaccines, but they were an independent body and couldn't be rushed. All the facts that ministers should have been saying, but with the politics stripped out. Who knows? Experts might even catch on post-Brexit after all.

Mordaunt goes through the looking-glass and down a rabbit hole

10 DECEMBER 2020

It's been such a year of horrors that it's become easy to lose track of just how weird things are. But Thursday was one of those days when we slipped a little further through the looking-glass.

Only a year ago, many opposition MPs were still hoping for a second referendum on the UK's membership of the EU, on the off-chance that the public might have changed their minds. Now those same MPs are the ones pleading for the government to just get a deal – any deal, however crap – to avoid a no-deal Brexit on 31 December. Their expectations have fallen that low.

At the same time, most Tory MPs, who had previously bigged up the 'oven-ready' deal and openly boasted of a new trade deal being the easiest deal in the world and that a no-deal was unthinkable, are now urging Boris Johnson to go for that very same no-deal Brexit. No more mucking about with an EU that is stubbornly hanging on to notions of fish, governance and level playing fields – the same issues it has been going on about for years – and just leave on World Trade Organization terms. So we're in an upside-down world where Labour appears to have more interest in the government clinching a last-minute deal than the Conservatives. Go figure.

In the Commons there was a distinct sense of déjà vu, as, for the second time in a week, Rachel Reeves, the shadow chancellor of the Duchy of Lancaster, had secured an urgent question, asking her opposite number, Michael Gove, to give an update on the state of the Brexit negotiations. And for the second time in a week, the Govester declined to attend in person and sent his understudy, Penny Mordaunt, to do his dirty work for him.

And for the second time in a week, Mordaunt had precisely nothing new to say. Mainly because there was nothing new to say, but partly because even if there was, Mordaunt would be among the last to know. So she rattled through what she had learned from the 24-hour news outlets.

Boris Johnson had flown to Brussels for dinner with the European Commission president, Ursula von der Leyen, and had achieved as little as everyone had expected. Other than that, the previous day's deadline had been moved to Sunday. So in the meantime we were where we were, with the UK and EU still a long way from any agreement, but a deal was there to be done, provided the EU gave way on all their red lines. After all, it was the least they could do, given that the UK had withdrawn its threat to break international law in an agreement it had negotiated less than a year ago.

This was all a bit much for Reeves, and you could sense the despair in her voice as she responded. How come we knew more about what the two leaders had eaten – fish, followed by an Australian-style pavlova: nice shade there from the EU – than what they had actually said to each other? And how come Boris had returned and gone straight into hiding? Shouldn't the prime minister be showing a little more leadership by making a public statement to reassure the country that there were at least some contingency plans if the shit really hit the fan? What were the plans for the nation's security? After all, the EU had published its contingency plans, which seemed to amount to things getting steadily worse for the UK, up until a time when someone came up with anything better.

At which point Mordaunt lost the plot and started blaming Labour for the failure to agree a trade deal. In Pennyworld, Labour was guilty of treason for daring to hope for a positive outcome to the negotiations. The same negotiations she herself had just said she wanted to end positively.

Labour's crazy idea that a deal was better than no deal had completely undermined the government's position. By trying to accommodate a bad deal on the grounds that it was the least-worst option, they had somehow managed to make a no-deal far more likely. This was like blaming the Poles for the German invasion of Poland in 1939. At times like this, satire is pointless. Just transcribing the lunacy is more absurd than anything I could possibly make up.

'We all want a deal,' said Labour's Hilary Benn. Only it was increasingly clear that wasn't true, as Tory after Tory stood up to say they would be far happier with no deal and that they would be devastated by any deal other than one that entailed the EU capitulating on all its demands. It's yet to dawn on them that the whole point of a trade deal is that it inevitably involves external governance and a loss of sovereignty, but that these losses are outweighed by the gains.

Thereafter we slid further and further down the rabbit hole. Labour's Bill Esterson wondered if we could have an economic impact assessment of any deal with the EU that we turned down, just so we could compare it to the 2% loss in GDP that the Office for Budget Responsibility was predicting for a no-deal. Just so that we could have a sliding-doors moment when we could see how much better life might be without lorries full of food and medicines parked up on the French border. Mordaunt didn't think this was a good idea. Far better to jump into a no-deal without any regrets.

Almost as an afterthought, Mordaunt added that Sunday might not actually be the final deadline after all. We might decide to carry on talking pointlessly up until 31 December, because that might make the end of the transition even more dramatic. If no less inevitable.

Either Mordaunt was lying to herself and the Commons or she is a wee bit dim if she thinks the EU is going to significantly change its position in the next three weeks. So the thought lingered that Reeves and Mordaunt would be back next Monday with the same urgent question and the same lack of answers. And if that doesn't give you nightmares, it does me.

* * *

On 8 December, Margaret Keenan became the first person in the world to receive the coronavirus vaccine. Appropriately enough, the second person was a William Shakespeare. But that was pretty much the end of the good news for the rest of the month, with the government consistently seen to be on the back foot as Boris Johnson dithered and delayed in his response to the rapidly increasing number of cases of Covid-19, and the discovery of the Kent variant in particular. As most people had predicted, the regional tiered lockdown system proved hopelessly ineffective, with London moving from tier 3 to tier 4 in the course of just three days, still without any sign of the new measures having a noticeable effect.

Part of Boris's problem was that he was a good-time guy who hated being the bringer of bad news, so he was unable to level with the country about the scale of the problem – or that his own inability to act had undoubtedly made things worse and cost lives. Earlier in the month Johnson had promised that the country would be able to enjoy a normal Christmas and announced a five-day easing of the socialising rules over the Christmas holiday period. Yet by 19 December, he had been forced to revise this. People in regions that were in tier 3 would be allowed to meet in bubbles for one day only, while households in tier 4 areas such as London would be banned from meeting altogether. Typically, there was a delay between Johnson announcing the measures and them coming into force, so London's roads and railway stations became rammed with people trying to escape the new restrictions. And no doubt spreading the virus as they did so. On top of all this, the UK was due to end its Brexit transition period on 31 December, so parliament had to be recalled to pass the new trade bill that had been agreed with the EU only at the very last minute.

On Boris's big day, Tories kid themselves this is the deal they always wanted

30 DECEMBER 2020

Who would have guessed? When push came to shove, it turned out that a bad deal was better than no deal after all. The first deal in history to put more barriers in the way of free trade than the one that preceded it. A 1,200-page treaty and 80-page bill that was granted a mere four and a half hours of what passed for scrutiny in a recalled House of Commons to allow it to become law before the end of the year. In most countries this would be called a farce; here in the UK we call it a return of parliamentary sovereignty.

At least that's the way Boris Johnson was selling the deal to his eager backbenchers, who were all desperate to applaud his negotiating skills and brinkmanship, as he opened the debate. Such as it was. The sense of anticlimax was almost tangible, almost as if the Tories were also having to kid themselves that the deal was the one they had always wanted.

But this was Boris's big day out, and he was determined to milk it for all he could. It's not often he can just about claim to have delivered on a promise, even if much of what was in the promise bore little similarity to the earlier promises he had made. But then the truth has always been a moving target for Johnson. There was certainly nothing about an extra £350 million for the NHS each week. But then that bus left years ago.

The prime minister began with the good stuff on no trade tariffs or quotas and rather skated over all the potential downsides. There was certainly nothing on Brexit levelling up the UK economy: it seems to have slowly dawned on Boris that it had been 10 years of Tory governments and not the EU that had widened the equality gap in the country. Rather, Johnson tried to sell the deal as doing a favour not just to the UK, but to the EU as well, because it would mean that we stopped behaving like a country that was unhappy in the relationship and kept having affairs. It's not you, darling, it's me. So now we would be moving on to a more open marriage, where a bit of infidelity was tolerated. You got the feeling he's used this line plenty of times in the past. To round it off, he concluded by saying that no one loved Europe more than him, and to think of Brexit as a resolution rather than a rupture. Which hardly squared with Boris's years of anti-European rhetoric. But then consistency has never been his strongest suit.

In reply, Keir Starmer first declared that Labour would be supporting the bill, as the alternative of a no-deal Brexit would cause even more disruption and put more companies out of business. But having played the national interest card, the Labour leader did a quick recap of some of Johnson's lies – only last week he had given a speech claiming there would be no non-tariff barriers, when the reality was a bureaucratic pile-on – before moving on to the deal's limitations. Starting with the complete absence of detail for the service sector, especially financial services. The Tories had just bargained away 80% of the economy to secure the headline trade deal. The French and the Germans were laughing all the way to the bank. Then there was the lack of access to European criminal databases, along with a lack of recognition for UK professional qualifications. He could go on. This was the thinnest of deals, one that had only been reached through the UK's desperation to leave the EU before the end of the year.

Though she pledged to back the bill, Theresa May was lukewarm in her support, pointing out that she had had a much better deal on the table that would have passed if Labour had been prepared to back it. She had a point. To no one's surprise, the SNP leader in the Commons, Ian Blackford, said his party would not be supporting the bill as Scotland had voted to remain in the EU and Johnson's deal offered them next to nothing. He, too, had a point.

As the debate progressed, it became clear that Johnson had at least managed to achieve something no Tory leader had managed in decades: he had united his party – if only temporarily – over Europe. So it was job done for Boris, as Brexit had mainly been about divisions within his own party. It was just a shame he had had to remove all the talent from his benches and replace them with yes-men and -women in the process.

Even the Brexit headbangers of the European Research Group rolled over like pussycats. In years gone by, William Cash had been prepared to defend the British fishing industry and the integrity of Northern Ireland within the UK. Now he was happily prepared to sacrifice both. Northern Ireland could become a colony of the EU, and who gave a shit about fish anyway? Cash compared Johnson to Pericles and Alexander the Great. The rest of the Commons compared Cash to a man without conscience or qualities. David Davis, meanwhile, proved equally absurd, insisting that a worse deal with the EU was in reality a better deal than one where we retained the same benefits. Go figure. Liam Fox claimed that the Union would be stronger due to Brexit. It hadn't sounded that way.

Kevin Brennan was the first Labour MP to break with the party line by saying he would not be voting for the deal. His logic that parliament should be allowed more time for scrutiny by extending the transition period was impeccable. Up until the point where you remembered that Johnson was a career psychopath and would have taken the UK out of the EU on 31 December with no deal if he didn't get his own way.

Which was pretty much the point that Rachel Reeves made in her closing speech, as she reiterated Labour's support for what was a crap deal, pointing out the seven amendments it had tried to table in the process, as the lesser of two evils. Closing for the government, Michael Gove was his usual insufferable self. Smug, graceless, short of self-awareness – he somehow believes extra bureaucracy will make businesses 'match-fit' – and still prioritising point-scoring over trying to bring the country back together.

The session ended with a whimper as the bill raced through its second, committee and third readings at breakneck speed, passing by a large majority. But anyone who imagined that was the last we would hear of Brexit had rather missed the point. The lack of detail in the trade bill and the methods of conflict resolution promised a whole new world of pain. Months and years down the line, Tory MPs might not be so easily bought off if the economy flatlines. Boris had better watch his back.

To predict government policy, listen to Boris and wait for the opposite

4 JANUARY 2021

In hindsight, the clues were there for everyone to see. Last week, the government forced a vote on extending recess by an extra week until 11 January. After all, it wasn't as if there was a lot on for MPs to scrutinise. Brexit was bound to be going swimmingly, and the coronavirus was near enough completely under control. So sure enough, on the very first day of its prolonged holiday, Boris Johnson announced that parliament would be recalled on Wednesday.

It's now becoming easier and easier to predict government policy. Just listen to what the prime minister said in the morning, and the opposite is likely to be true come the middle of the afternoon. It's almost like clockwork – the government does what most reasonable people would have done several weeks earlier.

At every stage in the coronavirus pandemic, the government has been hopelessly behind the curve. From being late to lock down in March while the Cheltenham Festival and Carrie Symonds's baby shower went ahead.

From ignoring the SAGE advice in September for a second national lockdown and being forced into one in November by both Keir Starmer and the rapidly rising rates of infection. From announcing a five-day Christmas free-for-all in early December – everyone knew Covid liked to take time off over the holiday period – which he then had to cancel after everyone had already made their plans.

During the biggest national health crisis in 100 years, it's just our luck to have Johnson in charge. A man pathologically unable to make the right calls at the right time. The prime minister is a narcissistic charlatan. The Great Dick Faker. Someone who can't bear to be the bearer of bad news or to be proved wrong by people who disagree with him. So he stubbornly ignores the evidence until he becomes overwhelmed by it and public opinion has turned against him. He isn't just a liability as a leader, his indecision has cost lives. His hubris will only cost him his job.

So the day started off much like any other for Boris. A quick feel-good photo opportunity jaunt to watch someone get the Oxford/AstraZeneca vaccine on its first day of national distribution and a short clip to camera. Schools should definitely remain open, he insisted, apparently oblivious to the fact that most health and teaching professionals had said otherwise.

But Boris thought differently. Most schoolkids only got a mild dose of Covid, and the teachers should stop moaning. Despite the increased infectivity of the new coronavirus variant, teachers should take one for the team, as children couldn't afford to fall further behind in their education. It didn't seem to have occurred to him that children also have parents and grandparents with whom they live and who might not be so lucky.

There might be a time for increased restrictions – Nicola Sturgeon announced Scotland's early in the afternoon, and the Labour leader had made a second appeal in two days for Johnson to see sense – but now was not the right time. Which begged the question: 'If not now, then when?' With infections increasing exponentially, the death rate rising and hospitals struggling to cope with the rate of admissions, just how many more people would have to get seriously ill before Boris could be bothered to take action?

As it happened, not many. Because shortly after filming this interview and insisting there would be no No. 10 press conference that evening, Johnson announced he would be addressing the nation on TV at 8 p.m. Yet again, Boris had been shamed into another U-turn. Better late than never. Though too late for some.

For his TV address, a dishevelled Boris – why change the habit of a lifetime and make it look like you give a toss? – didn't look serious so much as scared shitless. Someone whose self-delusion had been penetrated by reality – temporarily at least. There was little way to sugar-coat the news, despite him talking up the vaccine.

No triumphs to be declared, no ersatz leadership theatrics for reassurance. Only the despair of a down-on-his-luck TV evangelist was on offer in the eight-minute statement.

He began as if the huge rise in coronavirus cases had come as a massive shock to him at lunchtime, even though it was old news to the rest of the country, and spoke of his deep regret – the hurt was all his – at putting the country back into a total lockdown. Including closing the schools he had opened that morning.

'Some of you might be wondering why we haven't done this before,' he said. A question literally no one was asking as no one expects anything but incompetence and delay from this government any more. Typically, there was nothing about financial support for those whose livelihoods may be affected. He ended by saying that if all went well, there could be an easing of the lockdown by mid-February.

But not even the Great Dick Faker, the master of self-deception, sounded convinced by this. As usual, he didn't have the balls to level with the country and tell us what we all deep down know. That it's going to take at least three months before there's even a hint of a return to normality. And that's if we're lucky.

'So we beat on, boats against the current, borne back ceaselessly into the past.'

Boris Johnson: a defensive man with much to be defensive about

13 JANUARY 2021

For the last few days, the Commons has been unusually tranquil, with ministers and MPs going out of their way to be polite and cooperate with one another. Partly because there have been so few people in the chamber that the theatrics lose their edge, but mainly because MPs of all parties are genuinely terrified by the scale of the coronavirus pandemic. Cheap point-scoring feels like a waste of time when people are dying by the thousands every day.

Needless to say, though, that all changed with Boris Johnson at prime minister's questions. It's not just the defensive, combative tone with which Johnson treats the session; that is perhaps understandable, given that he has a lot to be defensive about, and Boris's first instinct when under pressure has always been to lash out and blame others. What really sticks in the throat is the lack of regret and remorse in his voice. His inability to accept any blame for his government's response to the Covid crisis is borderline sociopathic.

Johnson began with a quick U-turn. On Monday, he had said there was no 'clamour' for 24/7 vaccinations. Now he was telling us they would soon be piloted. But it was when Keir Starmer ran through the recent government timeline that Boris resorted to bluster and outright lies. He appeared to have forgotten that Matt Hancock had told the Commons about the new variant two days before Boris had announced there would be no lockdown and Christmas would be going ahead as usual at PMQs. Since then, the government had consistently done too little, too late, and Johnson was unable to explain why this third lockdown was less severe than the first one, when the pandemic was now even worse.

Perhaps the weirdest exchange took place when the Labour leader moved on to free school meals, and Johnson merely accused Starmer of being worse at pointing out how crap the government had been than Marcus Rashford. Not the greatest defence of government policy. Keir had done his homework, though, and pointed out that the £30 free school meals worth about a fiver were more or less in line with the Department for Education's own guidelines. Give or take a tin of sweetcorn.

At which point Boris gave up on not answering questions and went into a long rant about Labour's failings that the Speaker had to interrupt and call to a halt. This hadn't been a vintage Starmer performance – he still struggles rather when Johnson basically ignores him – but it had been enough to expose most of the prime minister's more disturbing pathologies.

There were fewer hiding places on offer for Johnson during his two-hour appearance before the liaison committee – the supergroup of select committee chairs – as he faced more detailed questions on his handling of the pandemic and the UK's exit from the EU. Though obviously that did not stop Boris from engaging in his favourite pastime of endless pointless digressions designed to disguise his lack of straight answers.

Not that Johnson didn't appear to have made more effort to come prepared to this meeting of the committee. Now that Dominic Cummings is off the scene, it feels as if his new team of advisers in No. 10 have been telling him he needs to do more preparation for these events, and in particular just to be more polite and try to appear interested in what he is being asked. His standard response to most questions about coronavirus was that the vaccine will sort things out eventually. He had less to say on his government's track record over the past 10 months, as he has invariably done too little, too late. His desperate need to be loved by not imposing restrictions may well have accounted for thousands of unnecessary deaths.

When push came to shove, Johnson again disowned his own government's guidance on free school meals and agreed with both Robert Halfon and Catherine McKinnell that what had been provided by some contractors had been pitiful. He also appeared not to hear McKinnell enquire if he regretted having once said that Donald Trump should be awarded the Nobel Peace Prize. Perhaps even Boris struggles to believe he could ever have said anything so absurd.

Labour's Stephen Timms managed to extract an inference that the £20 uplift in universal credit would not be extended beyond April, but as so often it was Yvette Cooper who really managed to get under his skin. There is no love lost between the two, and Johnson is self-aware enough to realise that in a straight fight he will always come off worse. So he opted for damage limitation as Cooper challenged him on his lack of action on both the South African and Brazilian variants.

Right now, Cooper observed, it was possible for anyone to fly into the UK from both these destinations and travel onwards by public transport without a negative coronavirus test. Or indeed with little chance of anyone checking whether you self-isolated once home. Boris merely muttered 'We're taking steps' over and over again, before mentioning the vaccine once more.

After which the fait accompli of Britain's exit from the EU felt more like an afterthought. Hilary Benn pointed out that many supermarket shelves in Northern Ireland were empty due to the increased bureaucracy. Boris somehow managed to contradict himself by saying the flow of goods from Great Britain into Northern Ireland had never been so smooth, which was why goods were flying off the supermarket shelves, but that any ongoing problems would soon be sorted out. Let the good times roll.

Thereafter, the session rather petered out. Not least because Bill Cash was so full of praise for the man who had rescued the country from the evil empire of the

EU that the only question he could muster was: 'Please tell us why you are so wonderful.' Something Johnson was happy to do at length. After all, that is his favourite subject.

Thérèse Coffey's Zoom walkout leaves even Piers Morgan lost for words

25 JANUARY 2021

Thérèse Coffey is normally a glass-half-full kind of minister. Sent out to do the media round on Monday morning, she even managed to claim to LBC's Nick Ferrari that getting just 1,868 young people – out of a targeted 120,000 – into roles on the government's Kickstarter scheme had 'actually been a huge success'. I hate to think what a massive failure might look like.

But even the work and pensions secretary struggled when she came up against Piers Morgan and Susanna Reid on ITV's *Good Morning Britain*. Having first delivered the classic line that 'The best way to tackle this virus is to avoid contracting it in the first place' – no shit – Coffey made the elementary error of giving a direct answer to a direct question.

Other ministers have gone to great lengths to appear totally mystified and avoid saying why the UK has the highest coronavirus death rate in the world, but Coffey

just jumped straight in. It was because we had an ageing population and an obesity crisis. So it was basically
our own fault and we had it coming. We were living far
too long and eating far too much. If only we had all died
younger or half starved to death, then all of this could
have been avoided. The humanity in her response was
touching.

Morgan couldn't believe his luck. So what you're saying, he observed, was that we Brits were basically too
old and too fat. Whereupon the minister completely lost
it and accused Morgan of being insulting for repeating
back what she had just said. Only Coffey wouldn't have
it. Apparently, there was no link between an ageing population and people getting old, and a population getting
obese and being fat. Or maybe she was just irritated with
herself for failing to mention a succession of failures in
government policy that had considerably boosted the
mortality rate.

Whichever it was, Thérèse spent the next two minutes
trying to distance herself from ever having brought up
'old' and 'fat'. Morgan was just trying to twist her words.
What she had meant by 'ageing' was an important boom
in senior living. And by 'obese' she had meant that under
the Tories there was no longer anyone going hungry; it
was just a coincidence that the poorest people tended to
have the worst diets.

Realising that what she had hoped would be an easy
interview had turned into a car crash, Coffey just reached

for the 'off' switch on her Zoom call. It's one way of terminating an interview, I suppose. If not one generally found in the politician's handbook. Time's up, got to go, she said desperately before her screen went dead. 'Wow,' Morgan commented. Wow indeed. It's not often that the TV presenter is lost for words. It had been eight months since Coffey had last been on *GMB*. Don't hold your breath for another appearance in the next eight months.

How Coffey must wish she was sometimes let loose in No. 10, as Matt Hancock had a rather more comfortable time when fronting the Downing Street press conference. Largely because he had nothing new to say and because he was able to ignore any questions that felt remotely tricky. Rather, he – along with the deputy chief medical officer, Jenny Harries, and Public Health England's Susan Hopkins – eased his way through the 45-minute session as if it were a cosy fireside chat. A few harsh reminders that the virus was far from beaten and that people still needed to obey the rules, interspersed with the good news that more than 6.5 million vaccinations had been given and that the early evidence was that the vaccine was effective against the UK variant.

This was the ideal gig for the health secretary. Normally, he's sent out when there's a crisis of some sort going on. But now we've got so used to every day being near enough a crisis that when things stay more or less the same and the death and hospitalisation figures are slightly lower, then it's cause for celebration in No. 10.

Even though the numbers would have been considered completely terrifying if anyone had mentioned them as a possibility even a month ago.

Disaster has become the new normal, so when things are no worse than they were the day before, it almost feels as if a corner has been turned. And over the course of the pandemic, Door Matt has become quite accomplished at sounding reassuring yet resolute. Or maybe our expectations of him and other ministers have become so low we now mistake mediocrity for comfort.

It also helps when no one actually asks any tricky questions. Had Hancock been asked the killer Coffey question of why the UK has the highest global death figures, then he might have struggled. Instead, he was asked when the lockdown restrictions might be lifted – though no one mentioned schools – and was quite easily able to point out that it rather depended on when deaths, hospitalisations, variants and vaccines co-aligned. It appears the rate of infection is no longer part of the equation.

He also hinted that he was in favour of quarantine hotels for all arrivals – not just for those from areas with known variants – without having either to specify how many beds they expected to need or why the government had taken so long to come round to this idea. In fact, by the end Door Matt even looked as if he was rather enjoying the press briefing. For the rest of us, it had been three-quarters of an hour of our lives we would never get back. Still, there are days when Hancock gets an even break. And as Coffey will tell you, there are advantages to being dull.

Boris Johnson's Scotland trip proves essential to nobody

28 JANUARY 2021

Nicola Sturgeon couldn't have been more clear. If the lockdown rules prevented all but essential travel – she had banned herself from visiting a vaccination centre in Aberdeen – then it was completely out of order for the prime minister to make a day trip to Scotland to drop in on a testing laboratory in Glasgow and a vaccine production facility in Livingston.

Except that secretly the Scottish first minister must have been delighted that Boris Johnson had found time in his diary to dress up in a lab coat, get in the way of a cluster of technicians as he emptied some boxes, and bump elbows with various members of the army. Not so much Captain Hindsight as General Chaos. Because every time Boris comes to Scotland, the poll ratings of the Scottish National Party – or the Scottish Nationalist Party, as Johnson insists on calling it – go up a few points. The last 20 opinion polls have shown a majority of Scots in favour of independence.

As with Johnson's previous trip to Scotland, this one had all been done on a need-to-know basis. There had been no itinerary released prior to his arrival, because the last thing that Boris wanted was a whole load of pro- testers turning up to line the route. The prime minister's unusual mission was to go to Scotland to avoid meeting as many Scots as possible. If possible, he would go to three locations that had been pre-sanitised to make sure no one gave him a hard time and get back to London relatively unscathed as soon as possible.

And that's more or less what he achieved. Johnson popped up for a series of pointless photo opportunities, and his only moment of slight jeopardy was when he was forced to do the obligatory short interview for the TV news channels. Boris didn't get off to the best of starts by talking about all the ways the rest of Great Britain had gone out of its way to help the Scots. But then he pre- sumably saw one of his minders doing a throat-cutting gesture and was reminded that the reason he had come to Scotland was to highlight the mutual benefits of the Union. So he then came up with something rather more placatory about how wonderful the Scots were. It didn't sound completely convincing, but then Boris seldom does. Diplomacy and sincerity are not two of his strong- est suits.

Inevitably, the interview then moved on to Scottish demands for a second independence referendum. 'People don't want another referendum,' he declared, despite the overwhelming evidence to the contrary. They were fed up with 'pointless constitutional wrangling'. This from a man who had brought the UK to its knees with endless constitutional wrangling over Brexit and had taken Scotland out of the EU against the wishes of most of its inhabitants.

Still, that was nothing compared with the hypocrisy of his insistence that he 'believed in the power of doing things together'. At times like this you wonder whether Johnson takes everyone for fools, simply has no conscience or has no memory. Or all three. Boris has only ever believed in doing what was good for Boris. Collaboration is a one-way street for any narcissist.

Johnson just had time to dodge questions on Desmond Swayne's lockdown scepticism and 'the teething problems' of his sell-out of the Scottish fishing fleet before wrapping things up with a near-incoherent summary of his day. I quote verbatim: 'If [the vaccine is] approved by the MHRA, then we will have 60 million doses of it by the end of this year for the whole of the British people. And so it's a success for Scotland. Uh, it's a success for, uh, Britain and, uh, it's a success for Britain because it is a success for Scotland. It's a success for Scotland because it's a success for Britain.

'So, uh, I'm, uh, you know, it was very, very encouraging to see it. That's, that's . . . I may have done some other things as well while I have been here, although I can't immediately recollect what they are. It's been an action-packed day and always a joy to see you.'

This was the UK's very own Cicero talking. Sturgeon must be counting down the days until Johnson makes his next essential visit to Scotland. Much more of this and indyref 2 will be in the bag.

You can't fault Matt Hancock's work ethic – just everything else

11 FEBRUARY 2021

You can't fault Matt Hancock's work ethic. While most of his cabinet colleagues have used the pandemic as an excuse to slide beneath the radar, the health secretary has been front of stage almost every day. Whether it's been taking Downing Street press conferences, giving coronavirus updates to the Commons, threatening to bang up serial liars for 10 years – Boris Johnson and Michael Gove need to watch out – or freelancing as a spokesperson for tourism in the south-west of England, Hancock has been your man.

But it turns out that even that workload isn't enough to keep him fully occupied, as on Thursday he was back in parliament to outline his plans to completely reorganise the NHS. Perhaps anticipating what was in store, only three backbenchers were in the chamber to hear the statement, but Matt was profoundly unbothered by the lack of an audience. His eyes, which for so long have looked like hollow sockets, regained their sparkle because he was back in his element, living his best life as a junior account executive in a management consultancy. KPMG's loss has been parliament's gain. Or possibly vice versa.

Hancock shook with excitement as he began talking in tongues. No opportunity to talk corporate bollocks was passed up as he greedily took the credit for a restructuring that he said would 'support and challenge' something or other and 'reduce bureaucracy and improve accountability via the fulcrum of integrated care systems' – aka undoing some of the mess caused by a previous Tory government's attempts to reorganise the NHS back in 2010. Trying to un-fuck previous fuck-ups is an increasingly popular Westminster pastime.

Some might say that the middle of a pandemic was not really the time to embark on wholesale changes to the NHS, Matt acknowledged. But he begged to differ. What better time could there be than when hospitals were overstretched and staff were exhausted? Doctors and nurses would find the excitement of the reorganisation a welcome distraction from their workload, a break from the monotony of having to deal with record numbers of patients.

The shadow health secretary, Jon Ashworth, didn't sound wholly convinced. He rather imagined that implementing radical changes during the current crisis might be the one thing too much for most NHS workers. Besides which there might yet be lessons we needed to learn from a crisis that had killed more than 100,000 people and led to 200,000 appointments being delayed for 12 months. So just maybe it was better to put the whole thing on hold for a few months and see where we were in the summer. As for the rest of it, he would withhold judgement for now, partly because nothing could be as bad as the current 'competitive tendering' system brought in 10 years ago, but mostly because – much like the rest of us – he didn't fully understand exactly what Hancock intended to do. He'd reserve comment until the health secretary fleshed out his proposals in plain English.

'I'm taking that as cautious support,' Hancock exclaimed excitedly, almost restored to his old Tiggerish self, as he mistook a non-committal response for something more enthusiastic. Ashworth scratched his head and looked understandably confused. The chair of the health select committee, Jeremy Hunt, who was nursing a broken arm sustained while out running that morning, described the proposed restructuring as 'brave'. As in, potentially foolhardy. During his own stint as health secretary, he'd never dared to suggest such changes. However much they may have been needed. The Department of Health was littered with the bodies of ministers who had come unstuck trying to reorganise the NHS.

As so much of what he said was vague to the point of incomprehensibility – 'empowering front-line staff', 'embedding accountability in integrated care systems', etc. – Hancock was able to survive the session almost unscathed. Even though he never did get round to explaining how social care would be integrated with health care when the government had still to announce its social care plan.

But that was a minor issue. As was the fact that the video link to Labour's Imran Hussain went down before the MP had managed to ask his question; Hancock merely chose to answer the question he imagined would have been asked. In Mattworld, everything was going just great. His plan was a sure-fire success that was all but up and running already, and it was only a matter of time before he was acknowledged as the saviour of the NHS. Blessed are the management consultants, for they shall inherit the Earth.

A year too late, Boris Johnson produces a reasonable plan

22 FEBRUARY 2021

Last April, the UK's chief scientific adviser, Patrick Vallance, said that 20,000 dead would be a 'good outcome'. Almost a year on, with the coronavirus death toll now north of 120,000 and the government having twice bungled its way out of previous lockdowns, you can see why the prime minister might want to avoid making the same mistakes with his road map out of England's current restrictions. So for his statement to the Commons, we were treated to a rather different Boris Johnson from the usual one. A more careful Boris that was fighting the urge to make extravagant promises.

This time, he insisted, his approach would be dictated by caution. Though for a prime minister who was adamant that his approach this time would be driven by the data rather than the dates, his statement was very date-heavy. There was 8 March for the full return of schools and friends delivering dead letter drops on park benches. There was 29 March for the return of the outdoor rule of six. Non-essential retail, hairdressers – Boris's Dennis the Menace barnet is in urgent need of a rethink – and holiday lets on 12 April. Indoor hospitality and some larger events on 17 May. A return to normal: 21 June. There would be no escape for those hoping to avoid the disco night at the Lib Dem party conference.

Only here it got rather more confusing, because it turned out that the dates weren't set in stone. Rather, they were merely the earliest days on which the loosening of these restrictions would be considered. If the virus didn't continue to respond to the results of the ongoing vaccine protection figures, or a new variant put a spanner in the works, then everything was back up for grabs.

The dates, it turned out, were merely best-guess scenarios, and Boris wasn't committing himself to anything that resembled an exact marker of success or failure for coming out of lockdown. All he would say was that this time it had to be irreversible. He hoped. Somehow the use of 'hope' and 'irreversibility' in the same sentence didn't inspire much confidence that the government totally believed in its own road map. But it would have to do.

Besides, it was a lot more coherent than some had feared, and Keir Starmer was happy enough to give Johnson the credit for having finally come up with something sensible at the third attempt. This was not the time or place to go on the offensive, and having checked that Chris Whitty was now happy for all schools to go back on 8 March – by some accounts, the chief medical officer had not been so keen at the tail end of last week – the Labour leader restricted himself to asking whether the government would improve its financial support for those forced to self-isolate. Boris seemed almost disappointed to find he had – for the most part – the support of the opposition and morphed into a mop-haired Don Quixote tilting pointlessly at windmills.

For such a significant statement, it all felt a bit of an anticlimax. Partly because almost all of the contents had been pre-briefed, so there was no element of surprise, but mostly because everything did sound fairly reasonable. Whether the government stuck to its plans was another matter, but for now it looked as if it had finally got something just about right. It had only taken a year and many thousands of deaths, but it had got there in the end. Even its vaccination programme was the envy of many countries.

Long before the end, many Tory MPs were touting their constituencies as ideal locations for a summer holiday, and not even Mark Harper, the leader of the hawkish Covid Recovery Group, seemed in the mood to pick a fight with Boris over what he saw as an unnecessary delay in the loosening of restrictions. Indeed, yet again Johnson sounded quite measured in his observations that there was no such thing as a Covid-free UK and that there would always be a substantial risk when not everyone had been vaccinated.

It was a similar prime minister who took the Downing Street press conference later that evening. Though that was less surprising, given that he was flanked by Whitty and Vallance, his two super-egos. Scientists who bring out in Boris an urge not just to speak the truth, but also to recognise it. Who have curbed his instincts to buccaneer with people's lives. If only for the time being.

Better late than never, we saw a Boris who could pass as sane. Someone who could cope with the certainty of uncertainty. Someone who appeared able to learn from his previous gung-ho approach. Who would have thought that possible?

* * *

Throughout the pandemic, both Boris Johnson and Matt Hancock had consistently gone out of their way to praise NHS workers. On 5 March, nurses and other NHS staff got to find out just how much the government really valued them, when Boris suggested they receive a 1%

pay rise. With inflation taken into account, what the gov-
ernment was offering was effectively a pay cut. Johnson
couldn't understand why the NHS was making such a
fuss. All other public sector workers were getting no pay
rise at all.

Untouchable Boris? Bluster-busting Starmer could well put him on the back foot again

10 MARCH 2021

These have not been the easiest few months for Keir Starmer, since the unexpected success of the vaccination programme has had the knock-on effect of granting the prime minister a high level of immunity from any sort of criticism. No matter what Boris Johnson says or does, the Tories remain comfortably ahead in the polls. Getting party donors to pay for the Downing Street refurb? Not a problem. An unused £2.9 million media suite in Downing Street? Because he's worth it. Failing to disclose PPE con- tracts? No worries. Unilaterally rewriting the Northern Ireland protocol? Just a bit of fun.

So no wonder the Labour leader has looked as if he's been struggling at prime minister's questions in recent weeks. He knows that no matter how well he performs, nothing he says will alter the political narrative. So why make the effort? What's more, Johnson himself has sensed he is untouchable, barely even making the effort to acknowledge Starmer's existence, let alone answering his questions. Even before all this no prime minister had done more to devalue PMQs than Boris. Now, with his narcissism unchecked, he has become even more insufferable.

Yet whether it was Johnson's hubris or Starmer raising his game – or possibly a bit of both – there were signs during this week's session that maybe Boris has used up some of his reserves of goodwill and that he will have to work harder to justify his existence in future. The Labour leader certainly looked more up for a fight than of late as he opened with a question that was short and to the point. Who was more worthy of a pay rise? NHS nurses or Dominic Cummings?

Boris sensed trouble and started waffling about how no one had done more for nurses than him – then again, no one had done less – and that they should be grateful for 1%, when other public sector workers were getting nothing. He was all heart. Starmer cut him short. The pay rise was effectively a pay cut, nurses were on average £800 worse off now than in 2010, and the prime minister had had no trouble fixing a 40% rise for his former adviser.

Now things began to turn surreal, with Johnson claiming that what nurses really wanted wasn't more money so much as more colleagues with whom to moan about how badly paid they were. After all, what was the point in working long hours for little money if you didn't have other workmates with whom to share the pain?

With every word Boris uttered you could sense confidence returning to the Labour leader. This was the old Johnson, the one who couldn't be bothered to prepare properly, the one who struggled to show empathy. This was the PM who was not nearly as intellectually agile as he liked to believe.

The longer the exchanges went on, the more convincing Keir sounded and the more feeble Boris's bluster became. This felt like a rebooted Labour leader. Starmer 2.0. One who had the best soundbites and was still hungry to accumulate even the marginal gains of an easy win at PMQs.

And wins didn't come much easier than this. Every Tory backbencher knows that the government is out of step with public opinion and that it will have raise its pay offer to the nurses, so it is increasingly painful having a leader who, as with free school meals, stubbornly refuses to bow to the inevitable and change course.

Starmer did miss a trick, however, by twice failing to pick up on Johnson's accusations that the Labour Party had voted against the government's original bill to give nurses a 2.1% rise. It can't have been that he was taken by surprise that Boris could come up with something so blatantly untrue; after all, making things up is the prime minister's MO. So maybe he just had a massive brain fade and had genuinely forgotten what had happened.

As it was, it was left to the shadow health minister, Jon Ashworth, to correct the record in a point of order at the end of the session: Labour had not voted against the bill, it had waved it through at both the second and third readings.

It would have been a nice moment for Johnson to put the record straight but, sensing what was about to happen, he had timidly scuttled out of the Commons before Ashworth got the chance to speak. So we have yet to hear Boris apologise for misleading parliament. Or lying, as most of us call it.

Tory milkman delivers speech surreal even by Commons standards

25 MARCH 2021

It had gone much as expected when the Commons debated the six-month extension to coronavirus regulations. Matt Hancock had opened in rather lacklustre fashion, safe in the knowledge that there was no chance of a government defeat, as Labour had already committed to giving its support, and trying not to sound too condescending when dealing with predictable interventions from Mark Harper and other Covid Recovery Group lockdown refuseniks from his own back benches.

Yes, said Door Matt, he quite understood his colleagues' concerns, but the road map out of lockdown was not up for discussion. In fact, he couldn't even guarantee he wouldn't be back in six months' time making the case for a further extension, if some new variant or a third wave made further restrictions necessary.

The shadow health secretary, Jon Ashworth, had given a similar boilerplate speech in response. The bill was far from perfect, blah-di-blah, and there were still parts of it that were draconian, but it was still, on balance, necessary. So with a heavy heart and great reluctance, etc., etc.

Then into the mix came the Tory libertarian Charles Walker. Now Walker is a fundamentally decent man who first came to my attention in 2015, when he broke down in tears in the chamber as William Hague and David Cameron tried to strong-arm him into a coup against the then Speaker, John Bercow. But since then he has rather slipped under the radar, until today, when he sprinkled himself with stardust by delivering the most surreal Commons speech that I have heard in the seven years I've been sketching. Satire is impossible at times like this, so all I can do is transcribe what he said, while including some thoughts and comments in italics.

'I want to talk about milk,' he began, 'because in the remaining days of this lockdown I am going to allow myself an act of defiance, my own protest that others may join me in. I am going to protest about the price of milk.' *Why milk? We never got to find out. Not even if it was skimmed, semi-skimmed or full-fat.* 'Now I'm not sure whether I think the price is too high or the price is too low. I will come to that decision later.' *He never did get round to saying what he felt was the right price.*

'But for the next few days I am going to walk around London with a pint of milk on my person, because that pint will represent my protest. And there may be others who will choose to walk around London with a pint of milk on their person as well, and perhaps as we walk past each other in the street our eyes might meet, we might even stop for a chat, but I was thinking to myself, and I will continue to think to myself.' *What does this even mean?*

'What will their pint of milk represent? What will their protests be? Perhaps they will be protesting the roaring back of a mental health demon brought on by lockdown, perhaps it will be protesting a renewed battle with anorexia, with depression, with anxiety, with addiction.' *Time to go to Milk Anonymous.* 'Perhaps with their pint of milk they will be protesting the lack of agency in their life, not being able to make a meaningful decision. Maybe a loss of career or job or business. Maybe they will be protesting this country's slide into authoritarianism, or perhaps they'll be protesting the fact that we allow unelected officials at No. 10 to lecture us how to live our lives.' *Yes, but why would they too be doing it with a carton of milk?*

'There might even be people with a pint of milk quietly protesting that the route out of lockdown is too slow, or perhaps even too fast. You see the point is, these people can project what they like, what concern they have on to their pint of milk.' *But you still haven't explained about the milk.* 'My protest, as I said, it will be about none of those things, it will simply be about the price of milk, and as I said, for the next few days I will have that pint on me.' *But what about the price? And what if you drink half and chuck the rest away?*

'It will be of symbolic importance to me, and at the end of the day it will be warm, it will have separated. And I can choose whether to drink or pour it away because it will be robbed of its refreshing elegance by the time it's been in my pocket for 12 hours. And if I pour it away, that might cause people some concern, but it doesn't matter, because it's my pint of milk.' *No one was saying that it wasn't your pint of milk or that you couldn't do what you liked with it.* 'And it's my protest, and I'm not seeking people's endorsement or support in my protests. And you know I heard, and I listened.' *But what did you hear? Voices?*

'I heard and I listened to my honourable friend.' *Presumably Door Matt.* 'This will pass, my protest will pass, the pandemic will pass. And in years to come, I will be sitting at my kitchen table, perhaps with my wife, and hopefully my children will still want to see me, and I will break away from our excited conversation about the day because I will spot that pint of milk on the table.' *But what if you've poured it away and there's no milk to look at?* 'And that pint shall remind me that the act of protest is a freedom. The freedom, not a right, and unless you cherish freedoms every day, unless you fight for freedoms, every day they end up being taken away from you.' *Er . . . no one's going to take away your pint of milk.*

Genius or madness. Your call. Personally, I'd be for giving Walker the benefit of the doubt. He certainly brightened up yet another dull day in lockdown. This was politics on acid. And wouldn't it be just great if at the next PMQs, when Boris Johnson is failing to give a straight answer, the whole house rose as one, pint of milk in hand, in silent protest. 'Free the Milk One.'

Primal rage at PMQs as Boris the joker is unmasked

28 APRIL 2021

Not even a trained arsonist could have imagined such spectacular pyrotechnics. This was Dominic Cummings's wildest dreams come true. Revenge didn't come sweeter than Boris Johnson having a breakdown during prime minister's questions. And not just a minor hissy-fit, but a full-on disintegration of the psyche.

This was the Boris that the prime minister goes a long way to conceal. Normally we get to see the careful construct of the happy-go-lucky joker, but here he was stripped back to something much uglier: the primal rage of the narcissistic teenager who has been caught out and has no place left to hide. An anger made worse by the knowledge that, as so often, most of the damage was self-inflicted.

Even without the Electoral Commission having said it would be launching an inquiry into Johnson's redecoration of No. 11, just an hour before PMQs began, there was little doubt where Keir Starmer's attention would be focused. Not least because Dom had all but set the six questions up with his blog the previous week, in which he had broken the story about both the bodies piling up and the unorthodox way in which Boris had allegedly paid for his Downing Street refurbishment.

Starmer started with the bodies. Had the prime minister said 'piling up the bodies' or something like that after a row about the second lockdown last October? Absolutely not, Johnson insisted. And anyone who said different was a liar. Fine, replied Keir. He was only checking because several people appeared to contradict the prime minister, and it would be important at some stage to determine who was telling the truth. After all, it was an offence to mislead parliament.

The Labour leader then moved on to the decorations. The John Lewis furniture that Michael Gove's wife, Sarah Vine, had, earlier on the *Today* programme, helpfully explained had needed to be chucked out because someone as important as Boris couldn't be expected to live in a skip. With friends like Sarah . . . So who had paid the initial £56,000 invoice for the new soft furnishings?

Now Boris started ranting. 'I've paid the bill personally,'

he said. And it hurt. It was bad enough that he had been forced to take a major pay cut to be prime minister – how could anyone get by on £150,000 per year? – but it had never occurred to him that he would be expected to pay for his own living arrangements. Parting with cash was for the little people. And if he had ever suspected for a minute he would have to fork out for a £10,000 sofa, he would never have let Carrie order one from the posh catalogue.

Most people he cross-examined generally just said 'No comment' at this point, Starmer observed, before having another go. This time he tried multiple choice. Had it been the taxpayer, the Conservative Party, a Tory donor or the prime minister who had paid the initial invoice? Again Boris avoided the question by repeating that he had ended up by paying and he couldn't see what all the fuss was about. He might find that the Electoral Commission isn't so easily fobbed off by him answering a different question from the one asked.

By now Johnson was in full rant, oblivious to everything but his own fury and a burning sense of injustice at being asked to pay for anything himself. Labour had spent £500,000 on doing up Downing Street, he said, so anything he had spent was chicken feed. He already seemed to have forgotten about the £2.6 million he spent on a brand-new media suite that he's now too frightened to use in case people ask him any further awkward questions.

Starmer closed by listing the seven principles of the Nolan commission – selflessness, integrity, objectivity, accountability, openness, honesty and leadership – but Boris was too hysterical to take anything in. Instead, he got sweaty and just shouted about why wasn't he being asked about the vaccine rollout and other things that were going well. He even threw in a lie about Labour not having voted for the Brexit deal, just for the hell of it. A few Tory backbenchers cried out, 'More, more,' but most had the decency to look embarrassed.

This was always how it was going to be. Just as Cummings had predicted when he went public with his dirt. It was never going to be the big things that brought Boris down. The public could tolerate any amount of untruths about Brexit and incompetence at the handling of the coronavirus in the first nine months of the pandemic. That was all priced into the Johnson public persona. The Careless Dr Feelgood.

It was always going to be Boris that did for Boris. The sense that the country's priorities only took precedence when they happened to coincide with his own. And today we had seen that Johnson's actual priorities lay in self-preservation. The refusal to say who had paid for the refurb. The personal briefings to newspaper editors trashing Dom. This had shown the real Boris. The nasty, self-serving Boris. The Boris for whom ordinary rules do not apply. The Boris he went out of his way to keep hidden.

This wouldn't be the end of him. PMQs was too niche for that. But for all those who had witnessed it, there was a feeling there had been a seismic shift. What had been seen could not be unseen. There is a crack in everything. That's how the light gets in. The SNP's Ian Blackford used his questions to ask whether Johnson considered himself to be a liar. Curiously, Boris didn't answer. It was the closest he got to telling the truth throughout the session.

If Starmer wants to win Hartlepool, polls suggest he should stop visiting

4 MAY 2021

It's going to be a long old week for Keir Starmer. One which will be first spent trying to convince the country he hasn't given up on winning the Hartlepool by-election, and then, almost certainly, explaining why he never expected to hold on to the north-eastern constituency anyway.

The Labour leader's day had got off to a bad start with a Survation opinion poll, commissioned by ITV's *Good Morning Britain*, showing the Tories held a 17% lead over Labour in Hartlepool, a seat that had never gone to the Conservatives in its history. *GMB*'s Susanna Reid cut to the chase. 'Why were things going so wrong?' she asked.

'I've been to Hartlepool three times now,' Starmer began. Though maybe he might have been better off visiting less frequently, as every time he showed his face, Labour appeared to do worse in the polls. Starmer pressed on. It was jobs that were coming up with the voters he had met, and only he was promising to improve job security.

Which rather suggested he had been having different conversations from the ones others had been holding or that the people he had met had been humouring him. Because it looked to everyone else like either people had now decided they were quite happy with more than a decade of Tory governments or that Labour was still viewed as an anti-Brexit party and that those who had voted for the Brexit Party in 2019 were now planning on backing the Conservatives.

After Starmer had merely repeated his 'jobs, jobs, jobs' mantra, Reid asked him about the photo opportunity in the John Lewis wallpaper department. Why had he bothered? Starmer sighed. He had known at the time it was a bad idea – after all, only Boris Johnson was ever given a free pass on such lame political stunts – but now he was obliged to defend a weak visual gag as serious commentary on Tory sleaze and spending priorities by getting sidelined on to nurses' pay. Reid was unimpressed. 'Was it really that bad to spend money on doing up Downing Street?' she said. The *GMB* presenter clearly sees a future in sponsored government. Suits with Betfred logos, just like the snooker players. Nappies donated by Dyson. The possibilities were endless.

Reid's sidekick, Adil Ray, went for the jugular by going back to Hartlepool. If Labour did lose on Thursday, would Starmer consider standing down as leader? Starmer dodged the question by insisting the by-election was not yet lost. Hopefully, also, most pundits would spend more time dissecting the Scottish results than one by-election. Fingers crossed for an SNP overall majority. That really would give the Tories a headache. And besides, his position was surely safe enough for now. Did Labour MPs really want another leadership election so soon after the last one? Who knew which candidate the members might choose next time round?

Things didn't get any more comfortable for Starmer an hour later, when he was interviewed by Mishal Husain on the *Today* programme. Did he accept that Thursday's results would be a reflection of his leadership? He did. In which case, Husain said, if the dismal results of the 2019 general election were down to a combination of Jeremy Corbyn and Brexit, to what would he attribute the loss of Hartlepool?

'My job is to win the next general election,' he said, carefully sidestepping the question. 'We have a mountain to climb and we're climbing it.' Only Starmer currently gives the impression of someone who is doing more sliding down than climbing up. But then maybe you need a few falls before you reach the summit. Still, whatever the extenuating circumstances of there being no Brexit Party candidate to split the Tory vote this time round, no one really expected Labour to be going backwards from its 2019 position.

Er, yes, Husain observed. But we're talking about a seat that Labour has always held. Surely it was blindingly obvious the polls indicated that the punters didn't give a toss about sleaze and broken promises. They were happy enough for Johnson to do what he liked and to have caused the deaths of thousands of people from his mishandling of the coronavirus response in the early months of the pandemic. The vaccine rollout was going just fine, and they were prepared to go along with the Tories' 'levelling-up' agenda, even if they didn't really believe it would ever happen. Boris was successfully selling a vision. Even if it turned out to be a Ponzi scheme. So where were Labour's big transformational ideas?

'And fifthly . . .' said Starmer, having run through four other plans for the future. Somehow, even when he was trying to share his dream, he managed to find a form of language to disengage his listeners. Before he could get to sixthly, Husain switched the subject. Focus groups saw him as an aloof 'Mighty Eagle', soaring above the political battleground. So what could he say about himself that might surprise voters?

This was the time for Starmer to let rip. To have shown some genuine passion about what motivates him. Or to have lied about making models of buses. Instead, we got the standard politician's response: that he liked meeting people. He couldn't have sounded duller if he had tried. Then maybe the one surprise about Starmer is that there is no surprise. And right now, that's not a vote-winning look.

So who are you again? Boris Johnson meets the new MP for Hartlepool

7 MAY 2021

The real surprise was that anyone was surprised. Over the last few days, the polls had looked desperate for Labour, and it would have been astonishing if the Conservatives hadn't easily won the Hartlepool by-election.

And sure enough, those who had voted for the Brexit Party in the 2019 general election moved en masse to the Tories, and Hartlepool went blue for the first time since the constituency was created back in the mid-1970s. So what with the end of the Brexit Party and the vaccine bounce, the by-election had been an accident waiting to happen for Labour.

But part of the job description for any politician is to be able to look surprised by the entirely predictable, so it was inevitable that Boris Johnson would take the first train up to Hartlepool to do a quick victory lap. Though on arrival he was unnerved by one member of the welcoming committee. 'Who's that woman hanging around in the background?' he asked the Tory party chair, Amanda Milling.

'That's Jill Mortimer,' Milling had replied.

'Who is she?'

'The new Conservative MP.'

'Cripes. Thanks for letting me know.'

'No problem. No one in Hartlepool really knows who she is either. She doesn't come from round here, and her whole campaign was based on knowing next to nothing about the constituency.'

'So how did she win?'

'Because she wasn't representing Labour and, un-believably, the Labour candidate was even worse. Now do try not to gloat too much as it's not a great look. You're here to look humble and promise to deliver whatever it was we promised to deliver on.'

Half an hour or so later, Boris stopped to do a brief interview with Sky as he walked along the seafront. Was it really such a shock to have won the by-election, given the demise of the Brexit Party and the vaccine bounce? Absolutely, said Johnson, somehow managing to sound sincere. The margin of victory had caught even him by surprise. Though he was delighted that voters had seen that the Conservatives had succeeded in getting Brexit done, and he was now determined to deliver on his prom-ise to level up across the country.

Just as soon as he had worked out what levelling-up

meant. The fact that levelling-up and offering equality of opportunity were things that every government in the last 50 years had promised and failed to do was rather beside the point. For reasons that even Boris couldn't quite fathom, voters seemed to trust him. Which was more than could be said for most of his family. To not know him is to love him. His friends were sick of his stories; the rest of the country seemed unable to get enough of them.

'Are you sure you don't have a question for Jill?' Johnson said, as the interview wound to a close. Er, no. No one wanted to speak to Jill. And no one seemed more pleased about that than Jill herself. She hadn't had much to say in the campaign, and she had nothing to add to that now.

Back in London, things were going from bad to worse for Keir Starmer. It wasn't just Hartlepool where Labour had tanked; it had also haemorrhaged support to the Tories in the local council elections. Not so much a defeat as a total humiliation. And now he too was obliged to give his first televised take on what had been a disastrous set of election results.

'I take full responsibility,' he began. The Labour leader tried to sound bullish. As if he understood the problem and had the answers. But he looked crushed. Devastated even. He had been expecting a bad day, but this was way worse than his worst fears. He went on to say he would do whatever it took to make Labour electable again. But really he was out of ideas. Other than trying to reinvent himself as a populist who would promise to give the country whatever it said it wanted.

It wasn't a question of left and right, he insisted. Labour needed to stop quarrelling and face the country – something that might have been more convincing if the first response of the party had not been for its two competing wings to kick lumps out of one another. Labour also needed to reflect and understand. Most voters will probably be remembering that Starmer had said much the same thing when he became leader more than a year ago; but maybe reflection and understanding takes longer than he thought.

What Labour needed most of all, though, was a bold vision, he added. And what was this bold vision? It was this vision that was bold. Starmer didn't get any further than this as Sky News broke off the interview in mid-sentence to go live to Liverpool, where Joanne Anderson had been elected city mayor. It just about summed up Starmer's day. Wherever the bold vision was, it wasn't with him. For the moment, he had been downgraded to an irrelevance. It was going to be a long way back for him and for Labour.

No boasting, no gloating, Boris somehow remains on topic

10 MAY 2021

It wasn't the results in last week's elections that niggled. Nor was it that he had made a bit of an idiot of himself by effectively being forced to promote Angela Rayner just hours after he had tried to sack the deputy leader as party chair for her part in running such a rubbish campaign. Only the Labour Party could turn a reshuffle into surrealist performance art. Not least by elevating some MPs to shadow cabinet positions for which there was no government equivalent. Anyone for the Ministry of Silly Walks?

What really hurt Keir Starmer was that the Tories couldn't even be bothered to make fun of the shitshow. Anything was better than being ignored. It was one thing for Labour to be ignored by the country; quite another for the main opposition party to be an irrelevance to the government. Throughout the day the Conservatives used every opportunity to avoid intruding on Starmer's private grief.

For just about the first time anyone could remember, Boris Johnson remained firmly on topic as he – along with Chris Whitty and Patrick Vallance – held a press conference to announce that all systems were go for the third stage of the easing of lockdown restrictions in a week's time, on 17 May. Six people from two different households would be allowed to meet up indoors; hotels, B&Bs, bars and restaurants would reopen for indoor service; and even some judicious hugging would be allowed.

Unusually, there were also no signs of gloating in the prime minister's opening remarks. No triumphalist reminders that though he had set out a road map to escape lockdown based on data, not dates, the dates he had picked had turned out to be the right ones all along. Perhaps the message from his advisers that boasting is a bad look has finally sunk in. Maybe Boris can't even quite believe his luck that the vaccine programme has been so effective and that he has finally got something right after all last year's mistakes that cost many thousands of lives.

Or perhaps he is having second thoughts about the country being ready for its final return to normality on 21 June. That certainly seemed the most likely as Johnson was asked if he might consider bringing forward the June date, if the data allowed. Absolutely not, the prime minister said. This third stage was a significant relaxation of the regulations, and it was important to proceed cautiously. A word normally anathema to Boris.

There was also a change in the use of language. Previously, he has always spoken of the irreversibility of the easing of lockdown regulations. Now he introduced the qualifier 'hopefully'. Earlier in the year, we had been offered a road map set in stone. Now we were being warmed up for the possibility of another lockdown later in the year. An idea Whitty was keen to reinforce. Things can come out of a blue sky, he said. Although the present variants seemed to respond well to the vaccines, there was always the possibility of a mutant strain that didn't. In which case all bets were off.

So which people was the prime minister keenest to hug first? asked ITV's Romilly Weeks. For the first time, Johnson looked mildly uncomfortable. 'Whoever I hug will be done with caution and restraint,' he said defensively. Advice that he hoped others would follow. Nor would he commit to whether he would be shaking hands with anyone. Still, it would be nice one day to get an eye-witness account from a visitor to his No. 10 flat to find out if the money spent on the Lulu Lytle soft furnishings was good value.

For much of the rest of the presser, Boris was content to either repeat himself or prevaricate. He had had some wonderful conversations with the leaders of the devolved administrations, and they had all agreed that the most important thing was to get Covid sorted. From 'Get Brexit Done' to 'Get Covid Done'. Weirdly, the subject of independence didn't come up once. 'I know, I know,' he had said. It had taken him by surprise too. But there we were. He had been only too happy to talk about independence, but Nicola had never mentioned it. So he had thought it best to keep off the subject.

The final question was on Tuesday's Queen's Speech. How come the government was planning to introduce photographic voter ID, when voter fraud had never been a big issue in British elections? There had been just one instance at the last general election. So could it possibly be because Labour voters were less likely to have photographic ID, and therefore would be unable to participate in elections? Absolutely not, Johnson insisted. That was an outrageous suggestion. Labour voters were now an endangered species, and he had always been committed to wildlife conservation.

Boris checked his notes and wrapped things up quickly. It had been tempting to make more fun of Labour's troubles, but he had been assured it was far more damaging for the opposition to be ignored and be seen to be talking to itself. And besides, he had dodged a bullet. No one had mentioned his Mustique holiday, which was now being investigated by the parliamentary standards commissioner.

As Hancock 'throws a sickie', Zahawi suffers a dose of the hotspots

25 MAY 2021

You're worried about the rate of infection in Covid hotspot areas. So what would you do? (A) Get in touch with local leaders and health chiefs to agree extra local restrictions. (B) Nothing and hope it goes away. Or (C) slip out some new guidance on the government website when no one is looking on a Friday night and express total surprise when local journalists only discover it three or four days later.

If you're Matt Hancock, you 'throw a sickie'. You've had enough punishment beatings in the House of Commons to last several ministerial careers, and you've no intention of showing up for another. So it was left to the vaccines minister, Nadhim Zahawi, to answer an urgent question from the shadow health secretary, Jon Ashworth, about the new guidance for eight areas of the country. Fair to say, that's an hour of Zahawi's life that will have left him feeling more than a little under the weather.

'Let's keep the politics out of this,' he began. Some hope. It was like this. The prime minister had mentioned as an aside in a press conference on 14 May that just because we were at step 3 on the road map out of lockdown, it didn't mean that people should stop being cautious. And any fool could see that what he really meant was that people should not travel in or out of the eight designated hotspots, which was the guidance put out on the government website a week later. So if the government was guilty of anything, it was that the techies responsible for uploading official advice had been a little slow on the uptake.

Understandably, this answer impressed few MPs on either side of the house, with many Tories clearly fed up that their constituencies had been put into regional lock-down without any consultation with them, public health officials and local authorities. And the angrier they got, the more Zahawi found he was unable to stop digging himself in deeper. Of course people could travel to and from Covid hotspots, providing they only did it if it was for something essential. Such as going to visit a friend outdoors over the half-term break.

Only that wasn't anything like the guidance on the government website, Ashworth and others pointed out. The official line was that essential travel did not include going to visit a few mates in their garden. And it was also completely opaque on whether travelling to school or work in an affected area counted as essential. When pressed on this last point by the Lib Dem Munira Wilson, Zahawi sounded shifty and evaded the question. Largely because he was just as in the dark as everyone else on this.

Labour's Yvette Cooper tried to join the dots for him. Were people from Leicester, Bolton and the other six areas allowed to go on holiday to countries, such as Portugal, that were on the green list? And wasn't the fundamental problem that the government had created the fiasco for itself by failing to put India on the travel red list until far too late in the day? Zahawi opened and closed his mouth but nothing coherent came out.

But it was the Tory MPs who inflicted the most dam-age. Though a few mates tried to come to his rescue by praising the vaccine rollout, most could barely contain their anger at the levels of incompetence on view. They certainly had no recollection of the prime minister effectively imposing regional lockdowns on 14 May and were buggered if they would let their constituents be treated with such disrespect. The guidance is just guidance, Zahawi said, desperate to appease them. So people were free to ignore it if they felt like it. Though obviously he would rather they didn't. Was that more or less clear? It was the new take-it-or-leave-it lockdown. He couldn't have looked more relieved if he had tried when the Speaker finally called time on his ordeal.

Still, the vaccines minister wasn't the only one having a bad day. In between trying to prepare for a prime minister's questions on Wednesday that could have some Classic Dom-shaped curve balls, Boris Johnson was trying to explain both why the report into Islamophobia in the Tory party wasn't a whitewash and why he would never have described Muslim women in burqas as letterboxes if he had known he was going to become prime minister. Because it's fine to splatter casual racism across the comment pages of the *Daily Telegraph*. Just not when you're sitting in Downing Street. Then you have to keep your thoughts to yourself and say nothing.

Dominic Cummings stars in his own jaw-dropping, grubby, delusional miniseries

26 MAY 2021

Not so much a parliamentary hearing, more an eight-hour Netflix miniseries. The one where a lone delusional narcissist drives into town to take revenge on a whole bunch of other delusional narcissists. With a bit of *Independence Day* and *Spider-Man* thrown in.

Dominic Cummings's appearance before the joint science and technology and health select committee always promised to be good box office, and it didn't disappoint. By the end of the session, the body count included Boris Johnson, Matt Hancock, half the senior civil servants in Downing Street, COBRA, Carrie Symonds and Dilyn the dog. Not forgetting Cummings himself. It's not in Dom's make-up to resist a self-inflicted wound.

The proceedings kicked off with Cummings blindsiding everyone with an apology. One he was to repeat several times during the course of the day. Senior advisers, such as him, had failed disastrously, and he wanted to say sorry for all his mistakes. He even sounded vaguely plausible.

His was a tale of hubris. The Dominic Cummings who was shocked to find there was a man called Dominic Cummings who had been the chief adviser to the prime minister. The man who could write esoteric 15,000-word blogs endlessly about why he was right about everything yet was unable to fulfil his basic job description. The chief adviser who was unable to advise. Whose position as the second most powerful figure in Downing Street was meaningless because his advice was consistently ignored.

Which isn't to say the apologies weren't self-serving. Cummings knows the rules of the game, and if you want to go on the attack, then it's best to first make sure you've covered your back. First in the crosshairs was the health secretary. Hancock was basically a serial liar who should have been fired back in April last year. Saying that patients would be tested before being released into care homes was only the greatest in an extensive catalogue of crimes, Cummings claimed. Dom – along with most of Downing Street – had begged the prime minister to sack Hancock on a daily basis, only for Johnson to refuse because he wanted to save him as a sacrificial lamb for the inevitable public inquiry.

Accusing a minister of lying was a serious matter, said the joint committee chair, Greg Clark, right at the end. Was there any chance Cummings could provide some documentary evidence? Dom mulled this over, before saying he would see what he could drag up. Though he wasn't sure it would be ethical to hand over all his private WhatsApp messages with the cabinet secretary. Thereby disclosing at least one of his sources. Mark Sedwill's heart must have sunk when he heard this. The grenade-tossing tosser had just tossed his last imaginary grenade.

But it was the revelations about Boris that were the most startling. Not so much the stuff about herd immunity, the mayor of *Jaws*, 'kung flu', wanting to be injected with coronavirus live on TV by Chris Whitty, rejecting a September circuit-breaker or letting the bodies pile high rather than have a third lockdown: all these had been heavily trailed. It was the levels of sheer incompetence that were gobsmacking. The deputy cabinet secretary who had barged in to conclude, 'We're absolutely fucked'; a cabinet that had ceased to function; and a leader unfit for office whose actions had cost the lives of tens of thousands of people.

Boris was basically an out-of-control shopping trolley careening from side to side down the aisles. A man who woke up without a plan and just reacted to whatever he had read in the papers. 'The country deserved better than a choice between Boris Johnson and Jeremy Corbyn at the last election,' said Cummings, apparently having forgotten that he had done more than almost anyone to get Boris into No. 10. There again, he also said it was crackers someone like him should have got into such a powerful position in government and that thousands of people could have done the job better than him.

Like most things with Dom, though, this needed to be treated with some caution. His insistence that he had been powerless was delivered with the swagger of someone who had once believed himself almost omnipotent. And his refusal to utter a word of criticism about Rishi Sunak was just baffling. To Rishi as much as anyone else. Right now, the chancellor could probably do without Dom's endorsement.

Even his trip to Durham had been misunderstood, he claimed. It hadn't been anything to do with him having coronavirus; it had been because of death threats he had received. Which made you wonder why he hadn't just told the truth during his Rose Garden press conference. It would have at least been more credible than the story he made up. There again, he also stuck to his story that the drive to Barnard Castle with his family had been an eyesight test. But that's the way Dom rolls. His can be a highly subjective truth.

So why hadn't the man who fantasised about having everyone exactly where he wanted them resigned sooner if he was so disillusioned with the government's handling of the pandemic? He nearly went in March, he said. And he should have gone in September. But something had held him back. Not the belief that Boris would change – he'd surely seen enough of him to know better than that – but the intoxication of feeling important.

Time and again, Cummings said he wanted to disappear from public life. Yet he gave the impression of someone who was loving being back in the limelight and was desperate for the session not to end. As if he only knew he was alive by the attention he received. Even if most of it was negative.

It had been by turn both jaw-dropping and grubby viewing. On balance, it felt as if some light had crept through the cracks. The families of the bereaved deserved better than truths carved out of a desire to settle some personal scores. But for now, they would have to settle for what they could get.

Blushing bridegroom Boris Johnson is not wedded to reality

9 JUNE 2021

Don't mention the sausage war! With Brexit a no-go zone despite the recent escalation in tension between the UK and the EU over the Northern Ireland protocol, Labour's official position on the subject appears to be to not have one. Hoping that the cold-cut war would somehow resolve itself and disappear, Keir Starmer chose to go in on the much safer ground of education at prime minister's questions. Though not before first congratulating Boris Johnson on having recently got married.

The prime minister didn't seem best pleased to be reminded. Maybe the thought of having had to pay for the ceremony and reception out of his own pocket was still too raw. Rather than accepting the tribute gracefully, he just stared down at the floor in embarrassment and ignored it. It's just possible that the man who, according to a recent profile in the *Atlantic* magazine, sees life and politics as a series of stories has yet to come up with a narrative for his new marriage. He wouldn't be the only one.

Though Boris does though have a story for the latest education debacle. Or rather, he has a fantasy. One in which Kevan Collins, the education recovery chief whom he appointed back in February, had quit the job because the government had fully delivered on his proposals and his work was done. Which isn't quite the way Collins or anyone else saw his resignation. He had described Johnson's decision to stump up just a tenth of the money he considered necessary for the extra tuition required to bring pandemic-affected students up to the usual attainment standards as totally inadequate and had jumped ship in protest.

All of which the Labour leader duly pointed out. Yet time and again Boris insisted the opposite was true. The tutoring programme was the biggest of its kind in the world. Which made you wonder what the Americans, who were spending 32 times as much per pupil, were doing with their money. He was investing £14 billion in catch-up funds. He meant to say £1.4 billion, but what's a decimal point between friends? Johnson also twice said that the tutoring scheme would benefit those pupils whose parents hadn't been able to afford private tutors through their own hard work. Rather implying that those who didn't have the dosh had just been too lazy to earn the money to pay for the tutoring themselves.

As so often, the exchanges between Starmer and Johnson ended in an impasse. Though the Labour leader clearly got the better of the argument, Boris's refusal to answer the questions rendered the whole thing pointless. You could sense Keir's frustration. Ennui even. There was a time when he believed that his forensic style of questioning could get under Johnson's skin and expose weaknesses in the government, but the prime minister has realised he doesn't have to engage with the substance because there is no parliamentary mechanism to force him to do so. Rather, he can indulge his passion for stories by inventing his own parallel narrative.

And it's hard to see what more Starmer can do to hold Johnson to account. Other than possibly to turn PMQs into a piece of surreal performance art by asking Boris to explain his education policy through the medium of interpretive dance. Or to ask him a whole load of open-ended questions about modern manners. For instance, was it customary to start a refurbishment project with no idea of how much work is involved or how much it is going to cost? Or since he had just been married in a Catholic church, did he consider his previous marriages not to have taken place and four of his children to have been born out of wedlock? Somehow this doesn't feel like Starmer's style. But until something changes, PMQs is rapidly becoming an empty and pointless exercise.

Things didn't improve when the SNP's Ian Blackford tried to shame Johnson for being the only world leader at the G7, which the UK is hosting in Cornwall this weekend, to cut his country's overseas aid budget during the pandemic. Boris merely shrugged the whole thing off as some sort of stunt cooked up by 'lefty propaganda'.

The SNP leader observed that this was the first time he had heard Theresa May – one of the many high-profile Tories opposed to the cut in overseas aid spending from 0.7% to 0.5% of gross national income – described as a lefty propagandist, and he talked about some of the aid programmes whose cuts would result in tens of thousands of deaths in some of the poorest countries in the world. Again, Johnson just ignored him by lying that the local elections had essentially been a vote on the aid cuts. He was popular, his policies were popular, and so he could do what he liked, when he liked.

There was no better illustration of this than in his reply to a question from Labour's Andrew Gwynne on the resignation of so many key advisers. We have always been bound by the ministerial code, Johnson said dismissively. Not true. Priti Patel has been found to have broken it. Boris and Matt Hancock have been found to have pushed it to its limits by a supposedly independent arbiter whom Boris himself appointed. And now Michael Gove is in the dock. But all this is water off a duck's back to Johnson. At some point he will come unstuck – like every narcissist, he germinates the seeds of his own destruction – but right now he's riding the crest of the vaccine wave and looks pretty much untouchable.

Johnson maxes out his credit with Tory MPs: 'It's 19 July, and I really mean it this time'

14 JUNE 2021

It hardly came as a massive shock. Indeed, given the surge in coronavirus cases over the past few weeks, the surprise would have been if Boris Johnson had chosen to relax all of the remaining lockdown restrictions in England on 21 June. But it was unquestionably a disappointment – to the prime minister as well as several million others. Boris likes to be the feel-good man; taking on the role of the sensible purveyor of bad news rather cramps his style.

So it was a somewhat subdued Johnson – it didn't help that he was still coming down from his G7 Cornwall high – who entered the Downing Street briefing room, flanked by Chris Whitty and Patrick Vallance. There was a time in the early days of the pandemic when the chief medical officer and the chief scientific adviser were ingénues who, unknowingly, frequently allowed themselves to be used as human shields for government incompetence. Now they have both wised up, and their presence was as much to make sure Boris didn't have a last-minute change of heart as to do the heavy lifting of explaining the science and epidemiology.

Not that they need have worried. For we were in a parallel universe where Johnson was actually keeping a promise. Normally, Boris doesn't think twice about not telling the truth – lying is second nature to him – but now he was delivering on a commitment. He had said he would follow the data, not the dates, and although he had never expected to make good on that promise – in his own mind the dates had always come first – he now found himself backed into a corner where he was obliged to keep his word. He made a mental note to not let telling this truth thingy become a habit. It was too inconvenient and much too much like hard work.

Boris began the press conference with the good news. The UK was already substantially more open than many other countries. It wasn't entirely true, but hell, he'd just come back from a fabulous weekend in Carbis Bay, where he'd got to hang out and relax with a dozen or so of the most powerful men and women in the democratic world. Restrictions? What restrictions?

Johnson then got his excuses in early. When he'd set out the road map back in February, he'd always known that easing the rules would be accompanied by more infections and more hospitalisations. He didn't seem to have noticed the slide that showed the current dominant strain of the virus to be the Delta variant. Something he might have been able to suppress or eliminate had he followed the data in April and banned all flights from India several weeks sooner than he had. And it still rankled that despite the delay, he still hadn't got to go on his holiday/ trade visit to India.

So here was the deal, Boris said, finally getting down to the nitty-gritty: 19 July would become the new 21 June. Only this time he really, really meant it. The 21 June date had only ever been an aspiration, but he was now going to spend the next four weeks in a vaccine frenzy to make sure that only something he couldn't now foresee – there's been a lot of unknown unknowns over the past 18 months – would prevent him from opening up the country completely.

In the meantime, though, he would throw in the consolation prize of allowing people to invite more guests to weddings, providing they adhered to social distancing rules. Quite how that was meant to work was anyone's guess, and Johnson had the good grace to appear confused as he explained. There again, he could just have been wondering why everyone was so keen on large weddings. One of the joys of his most recent bash was that he had had to fork out for only 30 people. And even that had been more expensive than he would have liked. He couldn't for the life of him understand why so many families tolerated so many liggers on the guest list.

Almost all the questions – the new GB News channel got one in on its first day out, even if it wasn't clear there was anyone watching to hear the answer – focused on just how certain the government was of meeting its 19 July target. And the longer the presser went on, the more certain Johnson became.

Yes, there would undoubtedly be more deaths along

the way, but somewhere along the line you had to decide what degree of risk you were prepared to tolerate. And Boris could sense that he had maxed out his credit with his increasingly vocal backbenchers, who were spitting blood that their leader had actually kept a promise to the country and wouldn't accept any further delays.

As Johnson walked away from the podium, he could hear Steve Baker humming the tune of *The Great Escape*.